1893 —

MW00588815

# MANNHEIM
# AND
# HUNGARIAN MARXISM

# MANNHEIM AND HUNGARIAN MARXISM

Joseph Gabel

*Translated by*

William M. Stein and James McCrate

Transaction Publishers
New Brunswick (U.S.A.) and London (U.K.)

Library of Congress Catalog Number: 90–40506
ISBN: 0–88738–377–7
Printed in the United States of America

**Library of Congress Cataloging-in-Publication Data**
Gabel, Joseph.
   [Mannheim et le marxisme hongrois. English]
   Mannheim and Hungarian marxism / Joseph Gabel.
      p. cm.
   Translation of: Mannheim et le marxisme hongrois.
   Includes bibliographical references and index.
   ISBN 0–88738–377–7
   1. Communism — Hungary.   2. Mannheim, Karl, 1893–1947 — Influence.
I. Title.
HX260.5.A6G3313    1990
335.43'09439 — dc20                                      90-40506
                                                              CIP

*This book is dedicated to the memory of the late Professor Jozsef Spielmann, my friend, eminent scholar, and distinguished scientist in the field of history of medicine and sociology, whose thoughts and ideas have constantly inspired me.*

— Ave Atque Vale

*For Huguette with my deepest affection*

*For my friends David Frank Allen and Michèle Allen*

# Contents

# Preface

Mannheim's fate in France is characterized by a curious contrast between the astounding modernity of some of his views and their limited impact on French intellectual life. One needs only to compare the substantial article by Lucien Goldmann on Lukàcs in the *Encyclopaedia Universalis* with the unsigned note, brief but intelligent, attributed to Mannheim. In the recently published *Dictionnaire des Oeuvres Politiques* (Paris, 1986), *Ideology and Utopia* is unjustly absent. Nevertheless there are certain indications that Mannheim's years of oblivion in France are coming to an end. His name appears more and more frequently in bibliographies — in those of Raymond Boudon's works among others — and the *Dictionnaire des Philosophes* (Paris P.U.F. 1984) offers an intelligent article on Mannheim by Remy Hess. It will not however be possible to speak of a genuine turning point in his French literary career until the day the windows of Parisian bookstores display a translation of *Ideology and Utopia* worthy of that name.

I consider that the work bearing that title, published in 1956 by Marcel Riviére (Paris), *is not really a translation.* It is very close to the English edition of 1936 where the "translators" — probably with Mannheim's implied consent — largely distorted its message in order to ensure its favorable reception by Anglo-Saxon academe. They succeeded in their objective; several editions of *Ideology and Utopia* have been published in the United States, and Mannheim's work had considerable influence in the Anglo-Saxon world. But the requirements of American academia in 1936 were different from those of French university life in 1956. The biased translation, which has become the key to its success among Anglo-Saxon readers, was one of the very reasons for its failure in France.

In 1936, the major themes of intellectual life in Weimar Germany were only starting to gain ground in the United States. The distinction well established in Germany between the sociology of knowledge and the

ix

*Ideologiekritik* was then unfamiliar to American intellectuals. Wirth and Shils therefore "translated" *Ideology and Utopia* using terminology based on the sociology of knowledge and American social psychology (*"Bewusstsein"* is translated "mentality") thereby obscuring the "demystifying" aspect of the work (the theme of false consciousness), which played a vital role in the original text. Moreover, the passages dealing with the problem of "rootless Intelligentsia" (*freischwebende Intelligenz*), one of Mannheim's most controversial theses which is indispensable for understanding his overall conception, was omitted from the French translation.[1]

A chapter of this book is devoted to the debate on this issue. At the risk of repeating myself later, I shall now take up certain aspects of this debate that typify the way Mannheim is misunderstood in France. According to Goldmann the *Intelligentsia*, which allegedly occupies a privileged position in the ideological debate, is none other than academia. The dangers of a basically "gnoseo-sociological"[2] interpretation of Mannheim's work are apparent: if Mannheim is assumed to be mainly a sociologist of *knowledge*, then it would seem logical that he should consider the "Intelligentsia" to be the *knowledgeable* social stratum, i.e., the academics. Seen in this light, Mannheim's theory of ideology is nothing but a "*pro domo* plea" (the term is Goldmann's) open to criticism and even irony.[3]

It is certain however that while formulating his theory, Professor Mannheim made no reference to his colleagues. He explicitly refers to "rootless" (*freischwebend*) intellectuals, an adjective ill-suited to university professors. His real model was probably the intellectual milieu of Budapest from which he came, a truly "rootless" one with a high percentage of Jewish intellectuals, often brilliant but frequently barred from academic careers. This milieu produced a curious form of "open" Marxism (for which I have suggested the term "Hungaro-Marxism"), more dialectical than materialist, more concerned with the problems of ideology and alienation than with those of economics, taking an opposite course to that of orthodox (sovietic) Marxism which is more materialist than dialectical and much more preoccupied with the critique of capitalist economies than with the problems of ideology.[4] From the standpoint of the sociology of knowledge, this "demystifying" trend of the Hungarian Marxist school is probably due to its central position at the crossroads of divergent and sometimes radically opposed politico-cultural influences that are mutually demystifying ("crossroads Marxism"). Mannheim is not only the principal theorist but also, along with Arthur Koestler, the perfect example of this crossroads phenomenon. The essential socio-historical role of the rootless Intelligensia is to offset the "normal egocentricity" of engaged political thinking. The erudition of university professors has nothing to do with that.

In my view this is the key to the astounding modernity of Mannheim. A certain degree of egocentricity is a permanent (and almost normal) feature of committed (ideologized) political thinking; militants rarely put themselves in the place of their opponents. Nonetheless, our era is characterized by a pathological exacerbation of this tendency. Fanaticism is an extreme form of collective egocentricity; it is by no means an accident that the important book on that subject by the Greek philosopher G. Oikonomakos frequently refers to Piaget, theorist of infantile egocentricity.[5] Egocentric distortions of political concepts such as "racism," "fascism," "left wing," or "right wing" are frequently stigmatized in the daily press. Mannheim has been called a "bourgeois Marxist" and not without good reason, as we shall see later. He is nonetheless first and foremost a "crossroads Marxist" and as such opposed to all forms of social egocentricity. This is, in my view, the essential meaning of his theory of the socio-historical function of the rootless Intelligentsia.

The high percentage of emigrants, naturalized citizens and Jews among the theorists of the problem of alienation and ideology is a clear indication of the validity of Mannheim's views on this question. Let us take for example the case of Marx himself, a hardly converted Jew who ceased to be Jewish without becoming Christian, a commoner married to an aristocrat, an eternal migrant, an accomplished linguist and polyglot. The author of *Das Kapital* is a perfect example of the rootless intellectual, and the de-alienating aspect of his doctrine—to which thinkers such as Lukàcs and Mannheim are legitimate heirs—was probably rooted in this situation.

The portrait I paint of Mannheim differs to some extent from the traditional one. Mannheim saw himself as a sociologist of knowledge and is known as such in the academic world, but a self-portrait is not necessarily an adequate one. His theory of the rootless Intelligentsia is the crux of the matter. Seen in the light of "Mannheim, sociologist of knowledge" this theory is reduced to a trivial statement: "knowledge is the best cure for ignorance." In the light of "Mannheim theorist of false consciousness," it appears as a pioneering one. By making a clearer distinction between the *critique of ideology* and the *sociology of knowl-*

*edge* than Mannheim did, I shall try to demonstrate that the heart of his work obviously lies in the former. When his outmoded writings on the sociology of knowledge are reduced to their true worth, a portrait of "Mannheim, philosopher of political demystification" takes shape, with close intellectual ties to Raymond Aron. In the ideological crisis that the world is now going through — while I write these lines (December 1989) a genuine political earthquake is smashing a great number of "realized utopias" — Mannheim as one of the outstanding critical theorists of the utopian phenomenon can still serve as a guide.

## Notes

1. Mannheim's famous theory of the role of the Intelligentsia in ideological debate was formulated in the chapter of *Ideology and Utopia* devoted to the prospects of scientific politics. This chapter is missing from the French translation of 1956, which is an unfortunate omission in light of the frequent ironic criticism of Mannheim's thesis. In sum, Mannheim wanted to grant the Intelligentsia the privilege that Lukács reserved for the proletariat: the accession to a genuine political consciousness. Goldmann — like Raymond Aron, before him — criticized Mannheim's alleged claims to privilege of the knowledgeable social class to which he himself belonged: university professors. In reality, that is completely untrue.
2. "Gnoseo-sociology" means sociology of knowledge.
3. Cf. L. Goldmann, *Sciences humaines et philosophie* (Paris: P.U.F., 1952) 38 ff.
4. According to G. Labica, ideology is a "suspicious concept, a sick concept, a doomed concept." See "Pour une approche critique du concept d'idéologie" in *Tiers-Monde*, XV, 1974:31 ff.
5. Grégoire Oikonomakos (Iconomacos), *Le Fanatisme* (Athens, 1961) (in French).

# MANNHEIM
# AND
# HUNGARIAN MARXISM

# PART I

## Hungarian Marxism

# 1

# The Socio-Historical Context of Hungarian Marxism

The success of G. Lukàcs in the postwar period brought Hungarian Marxist thought into the limelight. Its representative thinkers suffered the same fate as all Hungarian intellectuals, forced to choose between linguistic isolation from the rest of the world by writing in Hungarian or separation from the national community through use of a world wide language. One reason the school of thought which, on the model of "Austro-Marxism" I choose to call "Hungaro-Marxism,"[1] took so long to become established as an independent school is this paradoxical linguistic and cultural situation.

Are we entitled to classify Mannheim — who, though born in Budapest, was soon integrated into German university life — among the members of this school? The answer to this question depends to a large extent on one's definition of "school." I think that a current of ideas can lay claim to the status of a "school" if it offers one or more major permanent themes, provided that "comprehensive relations" (as defined by Max Weber) can be established between that thematic permanence and the socio-historical context. This sort of "gnoseo-sociological deduction" is generally painstaking. Goldmann managed it for Jansenism. We shall try to do the same for the Hungarian Marxist school, whose *demystifying* tendencies, according to our hypothesis, are rooted in the geographical and ideological centrality of Hungary — and Budapest, in particular — during the period from the historic compromise with the Hapsburgs in 1867 up to the Second World War. Since the various forms of collective egocentricity — socio-

3

centricity, ethnocentricity, Eurocentricity — are factors of ideological distortion, the centrality of a given socio-historical context can help produce nonideological, demystifying awareness. On the whole that is one of Mannheim's oft-quoted — and often misunderstood — theories concerning the *demystifying* role of the *rootless Intelligentsia* applied on a collective scale. From that point of view, prewar Hungary — Budapest, in particular — was in a truly exceptional situation. The multilingual, cosmopolitan atmosphere of urban milieus; the paradoxical situation of Hungarian nationalism, torn between monarchist loyalism and nostalgia for independence; the religious dualism; the divorce between the official intellectual life and counterculture; the gap between the capital city and provinces: all of these decentralizing factors favored the rise of a "Marxism of demystification" illustrated by such theorists as Lukàcs, Fogarasi, and Szende as well as Mannheim, whose work is the main object of my present essay.

To understand Marxism's appeal to certain strata of the Hungarian Intelligentsia in the first half of the twentieth century, it is important to bear in mind the fact that Hungarian intellectual life had never produced a great national doctrine in philosophy or sociology comparable to Durkheimianism in France or Hegelianism in Germany. That would not mean much in a country with poor or barren intellectual life, however in the sophisticated cultural milieu of the Hungarian capital city, it was meaningful in that it enhanced the chances of Marxism. A young intellectual of the *belle epoque* (before the First World War) who, in quest of a scientific understanding of social reality, would have turned to Durkheimianism in France, might very well have become a Marxist in Hungary.

Another important historical fact was the divorce between the official academic culture and the left-wing intellectual life. This split appeared some decades after the historical "compromise of 1867";[2] it was the dominant trait of Hungarian intellectual life until the Second World War. This phenomenon is typical of semi-authoritarian societies: totalitarian governments will not stand for the existence of an intellectual counterculture, and in democratic countries there is no need for it. I should like to underline the specifically Hungarian nature of this cultural dualism; in Romania for example, this phenomenon was less evident in spite of a similarity in the degree of public freedom in these two countries.

The destinies of the Hungarian psychoanalytic school offer a good example of this cultural dualism. With theorists such as, among many others, Sàndor Ferenczi, Géza Roheim, and Imre Hermann, the psychoanalytic movement of Budapest was, beyond doubt, one of the most important in the world. Despite that fact, there was never any question of granting Ferenczi or Roheim any kind of professorship.[3] In fact public authorities did nothing to interfere with the practice of psychoanalysis or the publication of its findings, but Academia was adamant in ignoring them. None of Ferenczi's or Roheim's young compatriots would have dreamt of submitting a Ph.D. thesis on a psychoanalytic topic at Budapest University. In such a context even well-to-do analysts, despite a brilliant social and material situation, would appear as intellectual marginals (*freischwebend*); this was especially true after 1920, when psychoanalysis began to attract Jewish medical practicioners who, being barred from major teaching posts, had nothing to lose. The convergence of these various factors resulted in the emergence of a sui generis gnoseo-sociological environment in which issues such as Marxist-psychoanalytical relations, or the dialectical aspect of the Freudian theories, were analyzed at an early stage.[4]

It would of course be an exaggeration to speak of a policy of intellectual coercion in prewar Hungary; the Horthy regime to a large extent respected intellectual freedom. But the Hungarian university of that time was a closed paternalistic world, which, at least in the social sciences, discarded all forms of modernity (this statement does not hold true for the medical and technical departments). For a young Hungarian of that time, being a Marxist in the theoretical field did not amount to a death sentence, even in the figurative sense of the term, but it certainly meant exclusion from the academic life. Access to higher learning was free until 1920, when the sinister *numerus clausus* law was imposed on the Jewish minority, causing an irretrievable brain drain. Academic recruitment had always been based on religious and political conformism. From the very beginning of his studies, the future intellectual was aware of the dilemma: either be a conformist and end up as university professor, or write in unofficial journals, acquire notoriety without official status, and live by one's fortune, pen or clientele. In the long run this situation produced a profound split between official and progressive intellectual life. I must add that, at least in the humanities, the latter attracted the most valuable elements. Marxism was naturally in the forefront of this alternative counterculture; the fact that its adherents were banned from higher teaching functions contributed to the emphasis of its antidogmatic attitude. This trend was to survive after the "Liberation of 1945" and create some difficulties for the left-wing authoritarianism succeeding to the right-wing one.

The isolation of the capital city from the rest of the country rein-forced that tendency. It is a rule that the capital is never the country, but nowhere was this contrast between the two more striking than in Hungary. To get an idea of the gap between the profoundly western-ized, high-strung, agitated, somewhat decadent capital, an incompa-rable center of art and culture, and the stagnant waters of the prov-ince, imagine New York or Boston moved to the middle of Nevada or to the Midwest, for example. The revolutions of 1918 and 1919 largely reflected the revolt of Budapest against the province; Admiral Horthy's counterrevolutlon in 1920 was a highly conscious act of retaliation against "Judapest," the cosmopolitan and supposedly anti-patriotic capi-tal.[5] Even in the most reactionary moments of Hungarian history, Budapest managed to preserve some freedom of expression—the pre-liminary condition of an intellectual life which remained brilliant even in the stuffy political climate under Horthy. Less than fifty miles from the brilliant, modern, and open-minded capital-city was the borderline of an archaic social world.

The theme of "Hungarian alienation"[6]—a vague feeling of fatality or of malediction[7]—is expressed with a remarkable vigor by the poet Endre (Andrew) Ady, one of the giants of Hungarian—and of world—literature. The Hungarian people are in the center of Europe, isolated from the surrounding peoples and languages. Their country is located on the historical crossroad of invasions, its history is a tragic one—a long series of unsuccessful revolutions[8] and interminable periods of foreign occupation. "We remained virgins on the heroic wedding bed of revolutions" exclaimed Ady on the eve of the democratic Revolu-tion of October 1918 (the "Asters Revolution"). Ady saw the fiasco of that revolution but died before he could witness the failure of the Communist experiment of Béla Kun in 1919. It is possible that the spectacle of this tragic series of aborted revolutions helped to sensi-tize certain representatives of the Hungarian Intelligentsia, such as Madách, Mannheim, and Kolnai, to the problem of *utopia*. A collec-tive feeling of solitude and failure can bring about diametrically op-posed results depending on the general level of political awareness. At a primitive level, such a feeling may give rise to a certain openness to right-wing-extremist ideologies.[9] In a sophisticated intellectual context — as is generally the case with intellectuals of Central Europe — it can, on the contrary, help people to understand the problem of alienation. I see here one of the gnoseo-sociological reasons for the distinctive character of Hungarian Marxism.

Two other important factors converge with the preceding ones as instruments of decentration: the paradoxical situation of Hungarian nationalism and the religious dualism.

In France, at least since 1789, there has been a solid link between the leftist attitude and the patriotic spirit. The *Front Populaire*, for example, was at the same time both a leftist and a patriotic movement. In Hungary, at least until the thirties, nothing similar appeared. In this steadfastly nationalistic country, nationalism was between 1867 and 1918 in a paradoxical situation. After the compromise of 1867, a "liberal party" came to govern the country. It was a traditional nationalist party that had no qualms about using chauvinistic language on occasion, but whose loyalist stance toward the Hapsburgs had quisling overtones that did not escape the public eye. The oppositional "Kossuth party," whose demands for total independence corresponded to "dyed in the wool" patriotism, could not reject, in the long run, the alliance with the Social-Democracy, whose uncompromising internationalism sometimes included overtly anti-patriotic overtones.[10] Hungarian nationalism at this time was torn between two opposite poles, both of which had a discrete flavor of antinationalism or, at the very least, "a-nationalism." Now it is well known — at least since Bacon and the *Novum Organum* — that idols of the tribe (i.e. collective egocentricity) are a powerful force in ideologization. Caught between these contradictory tendencies of Hungarian nationalism at this time, certain elements of the urban population were in a favorable position to transcend the "idols of the tribe" and corollary forms of false consciousness, such as ethnocentrism and eurocentrism, to name a few.

We find an analogous situation in the field of the religious experience. Hungary belongs to a minority of European countries with no truly dominant religion; Catholic and Protestant influences balance each other. Catholicism is the religion of the Hapsburg monarchy and of the majority of the population, but  Protestantism is that of an important sector of the Hungarian power elite. Moreover, Hungarian Protestantism is historically linked with the idea of national independence which for centuries meant a battle against Catholic Austria. The

Hungarian collective subconscious therefore lacked a system of universally recognized religious dogmas, which in countries with a single religion shapes even sceptical minds. Like the ambiguous nature of Hungarian nationalism, religious dualism promoted in certain milieus relativistic (and thus *demystifying*) forms of sociological thinking. When throughout the centuries one half of a population brands the other as heretics, that obviously creates an intellectual climate favorable to transcending religious alienation as such.

These factors were particularly influential in certains intellectual milieus of Budapest, which were drawn to Marxism because of the lack of a great national doctrine in philosophy or sociology. The result was a form of Marxism basically antidogmatic and dialectical, even relativistic, with some idealistic trend, to the extent that the primacy of dialectics over materialism implies such an orientation. Moreover this "Hungaro-Marxism" was above all *eclectic*. The *Galilean Circle* (Galilei kör) was at this time (before the First World War) the principal organ of progressivism among the students of Budapest. Its masonic origins did not prevent it from propounding Marxism and at the same time the philosophy of Ernst Mach, a thinker appreciated in Austro-Marxist circles but notoriously shunned by orthodox (soviet) Marxists. Béla Fogarasi who will become one of the most important personalities of Hungarian Academia after 1945, translated Bergson, another thinker unjustly ostracized by the Marxian orthodoxy. The author of the D*onnées Immédiates de la Conscience* influenced Lukàcs and indirectly, through Sorel, the outstanding Hungarian theorist of revolutionary syndicalism, Erwin Szabó. The first truly well-informed Hungarian specialist of Bergson, Valerie Dienes, was also a member of the Galilean Circle. Bergsonism, often branded in France as reactionary, was adequately perceived by a large sector of the progressive milieu of Budapest as a dialectical doctrine of de-alienation. The same holds true for Durkheimianism whose latent kinship to historical materialism was diagnosed in Hungary at a very early stage.[11] These examples illustrate the high degree of cultural openness and the ability of the Hungarian Intelligentsia at this time to synthesize. In that cosmopolitan milieu, open to every influence, resolutely anti-sectarian, and heedless of taboos, the problems of alienation, ideology, utopia, and even those of false consciousness naturally came to play an important role, not only in philosophy but in literature as well.

Let us consider two examples from opposite poles of this period, the first of which shows the early stage at which these themes took root in the Hungarian intellectual life and the second the tenacity of these roots. In 1860 the poet Emeric Madàch published his "Tragedy of Man," a grandiose philosophical poem concerned with the subjects of alienation and utopia.[12] Nearly a century later—at the zenith of Stalinism—a study of the Marxist philosopher George Nàdor was published under the title *Contemporary sophistry. A contribution to the logical analysis of the fallacious thinking of the Bourgeoisie in the imperialist era.*[13] This essay is a genuine critical analysis of a form of false consciousness, in the wake of the studies by Béla Fogarasi, which we shall discuss later on. Obviously, Nàdor—like Fogarasi before him—avoided the term "false consciousness" as a taboo concept; his examples are taken exclusively from "bourgeois" ideologies, and a timely quote from Stalin in the epigraph served as a life insurance policy that was far from superflouous at the time. Any reader the least bit alert could not help but recognize that the processes of logical distortion in bourgeois thought diagnosed by these two authors were identical to those underlying the Stalinist ideology, which was a "spontaneous ideal type" of false consciousness.[14] Considering the date (1952), the publication of such an article in a highly official journal is an event whose significance and implications need not be emphasized.

This tumultous period of recent Hungarian history was also marked by the blooming of an extremely interesting, nonconformist movement in art and literature, akin to some extent to the culture of Weimar but anterior as to its origins and independent in its inspiration. Between the two world wars, there were many exchanges between Weimar and the progressive Intelligentsia of Budapest. The modernist explosion in Weimar—the Bauhaus among others—was to some extent attributable to the influence of political refugees of Hungarian origin. "I recall with emotion," writes Frederic Karinthy,

> this era now closed forever, with its art full of grandiolquent mannerism, its messianic collectivism and disillusioned cult of the ego, its cynical sentimentality and cold-blooded search for the sense of the life, its naive complexity and sophisticated primitivism. . . . I recall with emotion this time since I am now aware of the fact that it was one of the golden ages of our national literature.[15]

Frederic Karinthy is worthy of our attention. Little-known abroad but extremely popular in his country, he was a genuine demystifier in the style of his English model, Swift, whom he translated, later writing a continuation of *Gulliver's Travels*. In his novel, *A Journey in Faremido,* Karinthy leads Doctor Gulliver through a world of intelligent machines. The description of that reified universe is curiously devoid of criticism: Karinthy's living machines — the Solasi — are more human than man himself. Obviously the author of *A Journey in Faremido* does not view reification as a totally negative phenomenon.

An analogous leitmotif underlies the essay of his excompatriot Aurèl Kölnai, *Eloge de l'Aliénation.*[16] Kölnai (1900–1973), who lived in London during the last years of his career, was an interesting figure in the intellectual world of the Hungarian capital-city before the First World War. He lived in Budapest until 1919 where he rubbed shoulders with the future representatives of what I call Hungaro-Marxism. Although he became a Catholic thinker while abroad and a staunch anti-Marxist, he retained a curious "critical loyalty" to the major philosophical themes of the intellectual milieu of his youth in Budapest. His lecture entitled *"Erroneous Conscience"* is a brilliant analysis of a form of false consciousness in the ethical field.

This outline would be incomplete without at least one reference to Arthur Koestler. This former Communist never completely freed himself from the influence of Marx; his criticism of the Communist ideology of this epoch could be signed, without any reluctance, by a Marxist of the Lukàcs school. A cosmopolitan polyglot with a nonacademic, pluralistic personality, the author of *Darkness at Noon* represents in my view a genuine idealtype of the rootless intellectual in the sense of Mannheim. He undeniably played the role of a critical theorist of false consciousness in the early postwar period, which won him fame and frequent hateful criticism. That is the common lot of demystifiers: the public does not like its illusions to be tampered with. Nearly a half century after the publication of this famous book, history has undeniably corroborated its views. Stalinism of which he was one of the most pertinents critics, has no more supporters. In light of what I have already said, it appears certain that the influence of the intellectual milieu of Budapest was to a great extent instrumental in shaping Koestler's personality as a demystifier.

This analysis of the socio-historical context of Hungarian Marxism does not claim to be exhaustive. I have simply tried to recreate an atmosphere. The "case of Lukàcs" belongs to this context; since I have already had the opportunity of speaking of him from that point of view, there would be no point in repeating myself here.[17] Goldmann cast doubts on Mannheim's originality with respects to Lukàcs; without going that far, it seems certain that the author of *History and Class Consciousness* had an undeniable influence on the author of *Ideology and Utopia*. The same holds true for three other Hungarian thinkers, highly representative of their milieu but much less known in France: Erwin Szabo, Béla Fogarasi and Paul Szende.

## Notes

1. I coined this term, "Hungaro-Marxism" in 1965 (*"Marxisme et Philosophie de Karl Korsch*," *Les Lettres Nouvelles* [Paris] [Aug/Sept 1965], 179). It refers to a current of Marxism of Central Europe centered on the problems of alienation, reification, and connected problems such as that of political mystification (false consciousness). It is mainly, though not exclusively, represented by theorists of Hungarian origin.

2. In 1867 a treaty was signed by the Hungarians and the Hapsburgs at the instigation of Ferenc Deák (the "Sage of the Country") which made it possible to reinstate parliamentary life in Hungary while keeping the House of Austria on the throne.

3. Sándor [Alexander] Ferenczi taught for a few months at the University of Budapest during the October Revolution of 1918, when the Socialist minister, S. Kunfi, tried to break this vicious circle by letting a breath of fresh air into the ancestral vaults of the University of Budapest. But it was a short-lived, inconsequential experiment.

4. I am refering to the *Triebsdialektik* (dialectics of the drive) elaborated by the Hungarian psychoanalyst Leopold Szondi, author of a well-known and much-criticized test that bears his name, and to Imre Hermann, Marxist and psychoanalyst, who only now begins to be known in France, thanks to the action of my late friend Nicolas Abrahàm.

5. That was one of the slogans of Admiral Horthy's armies in 1920: the "guilty capital," the traitor to the nation, must be punished.

6. This theme is reminiscent of the "leyenda negra" in Spain (Menendez Pelayo).

7. Cf. the definition of reification given by Lukács: "menschenfremde und menschenferne fatalistische Notwendigkeit" (a fatalistic necessity foreign to and remote from man) *Geschichte und Klassenbewusstsein* (Berlin: Malik Verlag, 1923), 141.

 8. "How beautiful it is to feel that one belongs to a people so imbued with fatality" (Ady).
 9. One of the right-wing-extremist sheets before the war had a characteristic title: "We are alone" (*Egyedül vagyunk*).
10. In 1849, Haynau ordered the execution of thirteen generals of the War of Independence. Ever since, the cult of the "thirteen martyrs of Arad" has been one of the great themes of Hungarian patriotism. That did not stop the Socialist leader D. Bokànyi (the future peoples' commissar under Béla Kun) from declaring around 1900 that the working class did not owe any respect to the memory of the "thirteen bourgeois" who had never shown the slightest interest in the proletariat. The Socialist poet S. Csizmadia would like "to tear out the slightest spark of patriotism from his children's hearts" (Z. Horvath, *A magyar szàzadfordulo* [The Hungarian fin de siecle] [Budapest: Gondolat, 1974], 600).
11. Cf. Oscar Jàszi, "Vérification inductive du matérialisme historique" in J. Gabel, B. Rousset, and Trinh Van Thao, *L'aliénation aujourd'hui* (Paris: Anthropos, 1974), 349–53. The original of the article was published in the review *Huszadik Szàzad* (Budapest). Jàszi considers the studies by Mauss and Beuchat on seasonal variations among the Eskimos, to be an "inductive verification" of the Marxist conception of the relations between the infrastructure and superstructures.
12. Cf. the fine article by L.G. Cigàny *Madàch* in the *Encyclopaedia Universalis* (vol. 10, 271).
13. This article of Georges Nàdor has been published in 1952 in the highly official *Annals of Philosophy (Filozofiai Evkönyv)*.
14. Both Fogarasi and Nàdor stress the importance of the "unwarranted identification" as one of the basic features of ideological distortion. The examples quoted by these authors are drawn exclusively from right-wing ideologies. There is no doubt, nonetheless, that the ficticious identification is a prominent feature of the ideology of Stalinism ("social-fascism," "Hitlero-Trotskism"). Our authors were certainly aware of the fact that their views involved an indirect criticism of the dominant ideology of this time.
15. The preface to the second edition (1920) of his collection of literary pastiches: *Igy irtok ti* (So That's How You Write!) (Budapest: Szépirodalmi Könyvkiadó, 1953), 7.
16. Cf. Aurèle Kölnai, "Eloge de l'aliénation" in J. Gabel, B. Rousset, and Trinh Van Thao, *L'alienation,* 257–67.
17. In Joseph Gabel *Ideologies* (Paris: Editions Anthropos, 1974), 121–22. The idealist tendencies of Lukács have been mentioned in order to explain his difficulties with the party as well as his reticence to acknowledge the primacy of progressive Soviet literature. That "explanation" is

an ideological smoke screen used to hide the real background of the "case of Lukács." Lukács was censured because of his role as a critical theorist of reification and false consciousness.

# 2

# Three Representative Figures:
# Erwin Szabo, Paul Szende, and Bela Fogarasi

After Lukàcs, Erwin Szabo (1871–1919) is probably the number-two figure in Hungarian Marxism, but he is as ignored abroad as Lukàcs is famous. He belonged to a generation prior to that of Lukàcs; his untimely decease at the age of forty-nine prevented his witnessing the shift of the center of gravity of the international socialist movement to Russia. He never emigrated, and his work is deeply rooted in the soil of his native Hungary. He was a complex figure all the same — a Marxist free of sectarianism and open to various cultural influences; an admirer of Nietzsche and Schopenhauer; at the least a good connoisseur of Bergson and all authors ostracized by orthodox Marxism. This cultural openness is one of the important hallmarks of the Hungarian Marxist school; it survived even in socialist Hungary's intellectual life. The non-Hungarian authors who most influenced Szabo are two libertarians: Sorel and Bakunin.

Szabo started in political life as a Social Democrat, but he soon left that party whilst remaining a personal friend of its leaders. He feared, perhaps under the influence of his libertarian readings, that the social democracy would fall under state control by participating in parliamentary struggles. He preferred to stay outside of the organization as a sort of external conscience of the party.

His works include a theory of imperialism which is, naturally, a little out of date now,[1] a remarkable Marxist analysis of the Hungarian Revolution of 1848,[2] a monumental critical edition of the selected

15

works of Marx and Engels, and a great number of articles published in various journals, including *Huszadik Szàzad.*[3]

This liberal — perhaps even libertarian — Marxist illustrates some of the typical traits of what I have tried to define as "Hungaro-Marxism." The Marxism of Szabo is an open one that does not reject any source of inspiration. He intended, however, to stress the Latin sources of socialism in order to counteract the influence of its German sources, which he considered to be harmful. Szabo believed that Sorel and Labriola would counterbalance Kautsky. German social democracy, with its theorists and politicians, was Szabo's pet aversion. Throughout his life he not only compared them unfavorably with Latin syndicalists but also unexpectedly at the end of his life with the British Labour party. History has in part proved him right.

As a "libertarian Marxist" the Hungarian disciple of Sorel was allergic to what we call today the "personality-cult." He was most certainly an admirer of Marx but not his unconditional supporter in all aspects of his political action.[4] In his annotations of the *Selected Works of Marx and Engels* he sided with Bakunin against Marx in reference to their historical conflict in the International. Szabo professed a curious attraction to the great opponent of Marx who was a genuine epitome of the *Tatmensch* ("man of action"), a symbol of the "will to the impossible" mentioned by Thomas Münzer. I wonder whether this attraction was not a symptom of some unconscious longing in the mind of this intellectual whose poor health kept him away from a too active political committment. It is not inconceivable that if he had not died in 1918, Szabo might have been tempted by the rhetoric of Mussolini.

A complex figure on the whole, Szabo was disconcerting in some respects.[5] Let me add one last trait. In 1917 Szabo was granted a flattering scientific mission by the Soviet government, but that scarcely dissuaded him from a reserved and sceptical attitude towards the "new path to socialism," although some of his Social-Democrat friends were seduced, at least temporarily. But Szabo was first and foremost a socialist opposed to etatism; he had a clear presentiment that the "withering away of the State," forecast by Engels, would after 1917, be long in coming.

What part of his work remains valid and of genuine interest? His history of the Hungarian Revolution of 1848 would, if translated, have few readers in the United States since the subject is too specialized. His economic studies are both pioneering and obsolete. For the socialist camp, this sworn enemy of state control and admirer of Bakunin was suspicious, but he cannot be overlooked, at least not in Hungary, since he influenced the marxist generation of which certain members rose to power after 1945. The *Selected Works of Marx and Engels* annotated by Szabo, were neither prohibited nor republished; in 1945 this work was still in circulation in the left-wing milieus of the capital. The history of Hungarian "1848," first published in Vienna with a foreword by Oscar Jàszi, was reprinted in Budapest in 1945 with a very different preface writer. Joseph Révai, a staunch Stalinist, expressed a severe caution:

> Every single sentence written by Szabo must be read with the utmost vigilance. He was mistaken about his syndicalist theory, his conception of the role of the party, his interpretation of the Marxist theory of the State,[6] his understanding of the development of labor movements, his evaluation of imperialism,[7] his explanation of "1848." His overall conception of the historical trends in the Hungarian labor movement is erroneous."[8]

A strange preface indeed! This edition appeared in 1945 when Hungarian political structures were not yet what they became a few years later. Moreover, the time when tattered copies of the *Selected Works* or *The Revolution of 1848* had been passed from hand to hand in leftist milieus, was still too near. For Szabo, the reign of Ràkosi was the epoch of forsaking ("la traversée du désert"). In the climate of intellectual liberalization that still prevails since some years in Hungary, Szabo has regained his rightful place in the history of Hungarian Marxism; his writings are once again published in Budapest.

I may have failed to bring to life the attractive personality of the first great Hungarian syndicalist; certains portraits must not be taken out of their frames. In some respects, Szabo is reminiscent of Sorel and of certain aspects of the theoretical works of Rosa Luxemburg, Max Adler, and Bakunin. A Marxist open to every cultural influence, a sworn enemy of sectarianism and deeply concerned with the ethical aspects of socialism, the Hungarian disciple of Sorel is a Hungaro-Marxist. His article on the prospects of scientific politics may have indirectly influenced Mannheim.[9] If Szabo were better known abroad, some of his powerful predictions might help Marxist sociology to adopt to the realities of post-industrial society.

Paul Szende (1879–1934), the "Galileist" secretary of the treasury of the Kàrolyi government, became a Social Democrat. What a strange fate: he might have become a great thinker but chose a militant political career, establishing a reputation as a much-criticized state financier and amateur doctrinaire.

The scientific works of Paul Szende are those of an intelligent, even brilliant, dilettante rather than those of a genuine social scientist. His documentation is sometimes rudimentary. He was first and foremost a forerunner. Too much has been made of Mannheim's intellectual debt to Lukàcs; the author of *Ideology and Utopia* also owed a great deal to Szende, although this is seldom recognized.

Szende started out as a historian with a study he had planned while in law school on the topic of Hungarian city life in the late Middle Ages. This first study was followed by several others on major Hungarian historical figures. Before becoming a Marxist officially, Szende was in fact a Marxist historian, but not the same type as E. Szabó. Szende was more interested in historical demystification than in demonstrating social antagonisms in the past. He tried above all to be a de-alienating historian. The official Hungarian historiography of his time, which was in general a highly distorted mirror, was in dire need of such correction. That concern continued to characterize Szende as an emigrant when he was totally captivated by the problem of political mystification.

He left Hungary in 1919, his emigration more or less voluntary. He had not participated in the "Commune," and as a technical minister of the republican government, he could have been pardoned. He lived in Austria, Czechoslovakia, and in France where he taught in the "College Libre des Sciences Sociales." He died in Paris in 1934.

His life in emigration had two focal points: his adherence to socialism and his studies of political mystification. *Verhüllung und Enthüllung*[10] is no doubt a milestone especially in view of the date of its publication (1922). It is probably the first Marxist study entirely devoted to that problem. Szende perceives history as a permanent competition between the ideologies of mystification (Verhüllungsideologien) and the ideologies of demystification (Enthüllungsideologien). This essay is a concise phenomenology of the latter. Eleven distinctive characteristics are identified by Szende.[11] I shall cite some of them: the apriorism of these ideologies, the priority given to form (Rangpriorität der Form), their dualistic (in modern parlance "Manichean") tendencies, and finally their propensity for reification.

All ideologies tend to become reified. Handed down from generation to generation, they end up having a constraining authoritarian form, from which thought can no more free itself. Abstract ideas, principles and concepts are transformed into essences or forces that are real though invisible and that are obeyed by humans as though they were superior beings.... It is understandable that Medieval Church denounced nominalism.... Its hostility to critical positivism is based on the very same motivation.[12]

According to Paul Szende the process of abstraction occupies a privileged position among the mechanisms of mystification; a propensity for the concrete characterizes the nonmystified political consciousness.[13] Every class, every nation has its own abstractions formed through the introjection of sociocentric value judgments that once made sacred by the group's consensus lay claim to the status of concrete realities. Robert K. Merton spoke, many years later, of the fallacy of misplaced concreteness. Gabriel Marcel claimed that the "spirit of abstraction [was] a factor of conflict."[14] Georg Gurvitch asserted that the dialectical method refuses any abstraction that does not take into account its own artificiality and does not lead towards the concrete.[15] According to Lukàcs, "the revolutionary principle of science lies in the supremacy of the concrete totality."[16] This convergence of different points of view is significant. Here we have all the basic elements of a dialectical theory of political alienation, and the personal contribution of Szende is unquestionably a pioneering one.

Szende also studied higher mathematics in order to take part in the debate on the theory of relativity seen as a typical Enthüllungstheorie. He was laying the foundations of a work with a promising title, *Mystik des Alltags,* when death struck him.

This is not the place to summarize the two major studies of Szende; some of his observations, though original at the time, have entered the public domain and might now, unjustly for him, appear as banal.[17] A painstaking search for his originality with respect to Lukàcs, Mannheim, and others is a sterile task. Mannheim seems to have taken a good deal of ideas from Szende; he also quotes him but perhaps not enough. Before Mannheim, Szende applied what Mannheim later termed "the general and total conception of ideology." Both these thinkers shared an interest in the problem of political mystification. We could say of Szende what we shall later say of Mannheim: this problem is the unifying theme of his work, the link between the historical studies of the young lawyer, the political action of the revolutionary minister, and the disillusioned reflection of the aging political refugee.

In contrast to Szende, the philosopher Béla Fogarasi took an opposite, much more picturesque path.[18] Fogarasi translated Bergson before World War I. In 1919 he delivered in the "Sociological Association" of Budapest an important lecture entitled *Conservative and Progressive Idealism* in which he challenged the classical Marxist equation "materialism =progressivism" and claimed for philosophical idealism the right to a progressive label.[19] In 1921 he published in Vienna a penetrating booklet, *Introduction to the Philosophy of Marx.*[20] At first sight this booklet appears to be vulgarization of the chapter on reification in Lukàcs's *History and Class Consciousness,* but in fact Fogarasi's book was published shortly before the outstanding work of his illustrious fellow-citizen. They belonged to the same intellectual spheres in Budapest which makes it rather difficult to decide the question of intellectual and chronological priority.

Between 1925 and 1944 Fogarasi contributed to various Communist monthlies.[21] He returned to Budapest at the same time as Lukàcs, where they both became professors at the University. In 1946 Fogarasi published a curiously split text, *Marxism and Logic.*[22] The borderline between dogmatic and liberal Marxism (between "materialisme dialectique" and "dialectique matérialiste" according to the witty formulation of the French sociologist Robert Meigniez) cuts here through the very same book: his dialectical premises, which involve a severe condemnation of authoritarian Marxism, are followed *in the same book*, by strictly orthodox conclusions. In this respect *Marxism and Logic* is no less significant than *History and Class Consciousness*. An English edition would be welcome on account of the originality of the author's views and the documentary value of this book for the history of contemporary ideologies.

The life work of Fogarasi and Lukàcs unite both major periods of the history of Hungarian Marxism: the heroic period before World War I and the period of the exercise of power after World War II. In the interim both thinkers were separated from their homeland's intellectual life by the necessity of emigration. I shall now sum up the situation of Marxist research in Hungary between 1920 and 1944. Despite a widespread opinion, Marxism as a theory was not forbidden during the Horthy administration; at most, it was banned from academia.

## Notes

1. E. Szabo, *Freihandel und Imperialismus* (Graz 1918).
2. E. Szabo, *Tàrsadalmi és pàrtharcok az 1948/49 es magyar forradalomban* (Social and party struggles during the Hungarian Revolution of 1848–49). A fundamental work published in Vienna (Austria) in 1921 and republished in Budapest in 1945 with a *very critical* preface by Joseph Révai.
3. *Huszadik Szàzad* (20th Century) was the official journal of the "Sociological Society." Founded in 1900 by intellectuals closely related to masonic circles, it was a center of French academic influence.
4. Szabo was director of the Budapest City Library, which continued to have one of the best collections of Marxist literature in Europe for a long time after his death (thus, right into the Horthy regime).
5. His attitude toward the Jewish question is one of the disconcerting aspects. But "antibourgeois" antisemitism was anything but rare in the progressive circles of Budapest, populated by converted Jews who made up a large number of the commissioners of the people in the 1919 Commune. The book by Peter Agoston, a law professor and a future commissioner of the people, *The way of the Jews* (1916), is one of the main manifestations of leftist antisemitism in Central Europe.
6. In another work by Szabo we find a pioneering passage:
    Our conception of the State also calls for a profound revision. . . . The lessons of the war confirm a henceforth undeniable fact: the primacy of economics, with respect to politics, is far from being the absolute that certain Marxists believed it was. The State is not a simple representative of the economic interests of the ruling classes . . . it appears rather, even in its relations with the ruling strata, to be an instrument of bureaucratic and political lobbies. In European capitalist countries it is no longer the bourgeoisie that is in power so much as the civil and military bureaucracy.
    (E. Szabo, *Imperializmus és tartós béke* [Imperialism and lasting peace] [Budapest, 1917] 43). That it is a highly unorthodox Marxism, Joseph Révai is perfectly right on that point. Erroneous or outmoded? That is a different question. Published decades before the studies of Rizzi, Burnham, and R. Michels, this essay seems a pioneering one. The Marxist Szabo poses an important problem related to the sociology of political power that the political Marxism of this time (Leninism), caught up in its myth of the delegation of class power to a party, has never been able to pose, and this for good reason.
7. "No matter what the the role of modern capitalism in State expansionism is, modern imperialism is nothing but a manifestation of a permanent feature of etatism in general. Independent of economic interests (and sometimes against them) States tend to enlarge their sphere of power by

virtue of the need to dominate common to all state organisms and even to every living being" (Szabo, *Imperializmus*, 36). These statements seem today trivial, but the quote dates from 1917! It provides more argument against contemporary imperialism — without excepting the imperialism of the "anti-imperialist camp," than the classical Marxist scheme, which is now definitely obsolete.

8. Révai, in the preface to Szabo's *Social and Party Struggles during the Hungarian Revolution of 1848–49* (in Hungarian) (Vienna, 1921, and Budapest, 1945) (with an extremely critical preface by Joseph Révai) 5–6.

9. Published in E. Szabo, "Lehetséges e tudomànyos politika?" *Huszadik Szàzad*, (January-June 1910): 133–36.

10. Paul Szende, *Verhüllung und Enthüllung. Der Kampf der Ideologien in der Geschichte*, Lepizig, Hirschfeld Verl. 1922. Partial French translation in Gabel, Rousset, Trinh-Van-Thao: *L'Aliénation aujourd'hui*, (Paris: Anthropos 1974) 319–48. A good article on Szende by Achille Guy, *Revue Internationale de Sociologie*, 1925, 79–82.

11. Paul Szende, Verhüllung und Enthüllung, 11.

12. Paul Szende, Ibid, 19 ff.

13. Paul Szende, "Soziologische Theorie der Abstraktion," *Archiv für Sozialwissenschaft und Sozialpolitik* (avril 1923).

14. Gabriel Marcel, *Les Hommes contre l'humain* (Paris: La Colombe, 1953), 114 ff.

15. Georges Gurvitch, *Dialectique et Sociologie* (Paris: Flammarion, 1962), 25.

16. G. Lukàcs, *Histoire et Conscience de Classe* (Paris: Ed. de Minuit, 1960), 48.

17. See, among others, his emphasis on the importance of *analogical thinking* as factor of ideologization. Later on Fogarasi spoke of "false identification," Alain Dieckhoff of "*équation perverse*" and Raymond Aron of "identification en chaîne." All these different terms refer to the same basic phenomenon: the reification of logic in the process of ideologization.

18. Béla Fogarasi started out in Hungarian intellectual life before World War I as an appreciated translator of French philosophical authors such as Bergson and Boutroux. As an independent thinker he was at this time a left-wing idealist. Director of the department of higher learning during the 1919 Commune, he was forced to emigrate after the downfall of the Communist regime. He returned to Hungary after 1945 at the same time as Lukàcs. Despite his notoriously "idealist" past he managed to escape the ostracism that struck his world-famous compatriot. His writings after 1945 are — maybe with the sole exception of *Marxizmus és Logika* —

strictly orthodox; they maintain, nonetheless, a high intellectual standing. In this period of his career Fogarasi became a Stalinist, but he never fell into the trap of "vulgar" Marxism.

19. "Konzervativ és progressziv idealizmus" (Conservative and progressive idealism), *Huszadik Szàzad* 1917 193–206. See Michel Löwy *Pour une sociologie des intellectuels révolutionnaires* (Paris: P.U.F. 1976), which includes interesting information on Fogarasi and the transcript of Lukàcs's intervention in the debate that followed the conference.

20. *Bevezetés à marxi filozofiàba* (Introduction to the Philosophy of Marx), (Vienna: Europa Verl. 1922).

21. These hard-to-find articles have promising titles: "Sociology of the Intelligentsia and the Intelligence of Sociology," *Unter dem Banner des Marxismus*, 1930; "Dialectics and Social Democracy," ibid. (1931): 359–75; "Reactionary Idealism," ibid. (1931): 214–31. (Tempora mutantur!)

22. *Marxizmus ès Logika* (Marxism and Logic) (Budapest: Ed. Szikra, 1946). The chapter on "false identification" (pp. 70–75) criticizes, on the basis of examples taken exclusively from right-wing ideologies, a logical process that played a notorious role in Stalinist ideology. The appendix to the work ("The Sociology of Karl Mannheim and the Dialectical Method") contains rather harsh judgments about the author of *Ideology and Utopia*, despite the undeniable intellectual kinship of the two thinkers.

# 3

# Hungarian Marxism after 1920

The paradoxal legality of *intellectual* Marxist manifestations under
Horthy can be explained by several converging factors. Unlike the
Communist party, Social-Democracy remained legal despite a dangerous period of uncertainty between 1919 and 1921.[1] This party was of
strict Marxist obedience; the fact that it was not prohibited ensured
the legality of Marxist intellectual mainfestations of different (Communist or Trotskyite) obedience. The repression which was severe,
even brutal, in the political field was rather moderate in the case of
demonstrations that were purely intellectual or considered as such.
The coexistence of very strong political and economic oppression and
a relative freedom of thought was the salient political characteristic of
the Horthy era.

Strange as it may seem, the Communist party, though strictly clandestine, was never denied some freedom of expression throughout this
long period. The novels by Sàndor Gergely[2] — which were party literature in the strictest sense of the term — were published legally. In
fact they were available in the public libraries. In 1927 Aladàr Tamàs
and Sàndor Gergely launched the journal *100%*, the name of which —
as internationalist as can be — leaves little room for doubt; it survived
until 1930. It was a top-notch, politico-literary review that was rather
sectarian and similar in spirit to the Soviet *Proletkult*. It featured a
series of theoretical works (Bukharine was one of the contributing
authors, under a pseudonym, of course) and organized avant-garde art
exhibitions. *100%* was replaced by *Tàrsadalmi Szemle*, a monthly that
was less literary with a less aggressive name and style, but was still

strictly orthodox.[3] Its two editors had very different fates. Doctor Joseph Madzsar, an eminent biologist and friend of Ervin Szabó, fled to the Soviet Union, where he disappeared in the great purge. His colleague, Paul Sàndor, a Marxologist and specialist in the history of ideas, published a work in French, *Histoire de la Dialectique,* which went practically unnoticed.[4]

In 1933 *Tàrsadalmi Szemle* disappeared in turn; the torch was picked up by *Gondolat* ("Thought") around 1935. It was far from being as aggressively sectarian as *100%*: the new party review was a distant, objective literary journal that fell right in with the spirit of the incipient "Popular Front." It did not disappear until 1937, on the eve of the Second World War.

The countries of the *Petite Entente* formed a buffer zone around revisionist Hungary. They included large sectors of the Hungarian population which naturally belonged to Hungarian intellectual life though governed by different laws. Czechoslovakia, an Occidental-type democracy, ensured complete freedom of intellectual expression. In Romania, with a very different, multinational context, the civil liberties situation was much the same as in Hungary, but the Romanian governments, as French allies, were happy to play the card of liberalism against Horthyist Hungary.[5] A Hungarian could be left-wing in Romania provided that he had a critical attitude towards the Horthy administration and since the latter was reactionary, that task was not an unpleasant one. Thus, the review *Korunk* ("Our Era") from Cluj incredibly managed to subsist between 1922 and 1939, passing through several periods of military censorship and the fascistic regime of Octavian Goga without even having to change its name. Under the brilliant direction of the Gàbor Gaal (who became a professor of philosophy in the Hungarian university in Romania after 1945), *Korunk* was one of the most broadminded Communist reviews of the time. Both scientific and literary and politically aggressive, though mainly with respect to the Hungarian administration, it featured articles by many left-wing Hungarian authors (under pseudonyms, of course), including Eric Molnar (known as Eric Jeszensky to readers of *Korunk*), who became Hungarian secretary of foreign affairs after 1945. This review, which had a great impact in Transylvania, was banned in theory but was readily available in Budapest; in fact it belonged to the progressive intellectual life of Hungary at the time.[6]

In Hungary itself the Marxist intellectual movement was not limited to Communist manifestations. The Hungarian social-democracy was Marxist; its official monthly, *Szocializmus,* was a review of Marxist sociology and politics. *Huszadik Szàzad* ("Twentieth Century") was banned after 1920 by the Horthy regime, but as early as 1927 the half-clandestine masonic circles started the review *Szàzadunk* ("Our Century"), a highly intellectual bourgeois radical monthly that was greatly interested in the questions of Marxist sociology.

Between orthodox communism and social-democracy there was a curious flow of ideas that was typical of the intellectual atmosphere of Budapest at the time known as the *Opposition.* One of its leading theorists, Paul Justus, was later to become famous as co-accused in the Rajk trial. The Opposition was a set of small groups that differed on sophisticated points of doctrine; its members included some remarkable connoisseurs of Marxist theory. In the circles close to the underground Communist party they were branded as "Trotskyites"; in reality, the genuine followers of L. D. Trotsky were a clear minority. It was not so much a Trotskyite as a liberal Marxist movement, profoundly influenced by the libertarian tendencies of Erwin Szabo whose works were widely read in this circle. The principal topics of the Opposition were a theoretical critique of the "construction of Socialism in a single country," a critique of the roles of the political party and of the state, and the problems of ideology and utopia. In addition to the libertarian influence (due to the writings of Szabó), this current of ideas was also shaped by other theorists: R. Luxemburg,[7] Karl Korsch, William Reich, Mannheim, and, above all, Lukàcs. *History and Class Consciousness* was passed from hand to hand. The opposition had its own periodicals, which were often short-lived; most of the theoretical work was carried out orally in seminars and on excursions. This curious ideological faction was important for two reasons: first of all, its was a continuation of the "open" tradition of Hungarian Marxism; and second, its partisans were ardently interested in the theoretical aspect of the problems. This characteristic interest of this movement in Marxist theory was both a response to the need for criticizing Soviet realities and a means of compensating their vague feeling of political ineffectiveness. In any case, the leaders of the Opposition, such as Paul Justus, were genuine scholars of Marxist theory.

If we include the Zionist movement, of which at least one of the branches — the "Hachomer Hatzair" — was resolutely Marxist, you will get an idea of the intellectual ferment that existed in Budapest under an authoritarian government.

Paradoxically, the balance sheet of the original contributions is somewhat disappointing. Paul Justus was an outstanding intellectual, but his personal contribution to Marxism is insignificant. Some theorists made their way abroad, such as the historian François Fejtö, who became an outstanding figure of the French intellectual life. The most valuable theoretical achievement of the Opposition was probably the annotated Hungarian edition of the *Introduction to the Critique of Political Economy* by Marx.[8] (This work was discarded by Marx and rediscovered in 1902 by Karl Kautsky, then published in 1903 in his monthly *Die Neue Zeit*). The text was published in 1931 in Budapest under a borrowed name; the lengthy notes were written collectively by the best theorists of this faction. The role of this publication was to use this Marxian text as a starting point for a Marxist critique of the Stalinist theory of constructing socialism in a single country. The idea of opposing Marx to Stalin was one of the permanent leitmotifs of the Opposition.

One of the noteworthy Marxist theoretical works of this time is *Materialist Ontology* by Aladàr Mod, published legally in Budapest in 1934.[9] Its inoffensive title disguises a far-reaching theoretical ambition: to provide a Marxist theory of all natural sciences two years before the publication of *Marxisme et Biologie* by Marcel Prenant. Aside from the inoffensive title, an obscure Hegelian style was intended to protect the book from the curiosity of the authorities; unfortunately it also protects it—and very well, indeed—from arousing the curiosity of readers.

In 1928 the Socialist party published a *Social Encyclopedia* (*Tàrsadalmi Lexikon*) a sort of *Britannica* for labor movements, in which Communist influences counterbalanced Social-Democratic ones. (Jozsef Madzsar, Communist and former friend of Erwin Szabo, was its editor; several Socialist MPs appeared among the contributors). This encyclopedia, which was a unique undertaking at the time, managed to justify Stalin along with Trotsky and Edouard Herriot along with Leon Blum. In fact, it foreshadowed the coming Front Populaire spirit, a noteworthy fact.

Exhaustive analysis of the literary production would require a special chapter. I should mention that there were many leftist Hungarian authors who, like Mannheim, were integrated into the progressive literature of Weimar and are generally thought of as Germans, such as Arthur Holitscher and Làszlo Radvànyi. In Hungary itself Sàndor Gergely (coeditor of *100%*) was a talented Communist writer; among the left-wing Socialists Lajos Kassàk (1887–1967) was the dominant figure. In poetry Kassàk started to develop a specific Hungarian form of futurism. A true genius dominated this period that was particularly rich in talent—the poet Attila József (1905–1937). Postwar communism in Hungary (the Ràkosi regime) laid claim to him; a doctored reedition of his sister's (Jolàn József) memoirs was published in Budapest towards 1955. But József was first and foremost a rebel. It is not hard to say what he would think today about authoritarian state socialism, were he alive.

In the late thirties the everyday life of this leftist counter-society grew more and more difficult. Political and even cultural repression became stronger and stronger. It first struck the Socialists, then the liberals and anti-Germans, in general. Valuable theorists and intellectuals finished their days in the terrible labor camps built for Jews. But Hungary never had book burnings—except, perhaps, during the brief period of insanity related to the sinister memory of Fr. Szàlasi, and that period was too short to allow the destruction to run its course. In 1945, when Lukàcs and Fogarasi arrived in Budapest to take up their respective professorships, there was no need for the new Marxist research to start from scratch: it benefited from a firm tradition with very real achievements. The "demystifying" tradition of Hungarian Marxism continued to survive, but in a semi-clandestine form. The debate on the "case of Lukàcs" attests to that fact. The most important continuer of this tradition was a thinker born in Budapest and transplanted to the free world of the Weimar republic, the "bourgeois Marxist" Karl Mannheim.

## Notes

1. In 1921 Béla Somogyi, editor in chief of the socialist daily *Nèpszava*, was murdered by ultra-right-wing officers connected with Horthy's milieu. After the elections of 1922, with twenty-five socialist MPs voted into the Chamber, the legality of the party was confirmed; nonetheless, contrary to allegations by Communists at the time, it was never "integrated into the system."
2. Sàndor Gergely (born in 1896) was a talented Communist writer with a

literary sensitiveness similar to that of Upton Sinclair. He was frequently harrassed by the Horthyist police, but his novels were never banned. In 1932 he emigrated to the Soviet Union.

3. This title was going to be reused in 1945 by the official monthly of the Communist party.

4. Paul Sàndor, *Histoire de la dialectique* (Paris: Nagel, 1947).

5. At the time of the execution in Budapest of the Communists Sallai and Fürst in 1932, several young Romanian militants protested to the Hungarian Consulate of Cluj (Kolozsvár). They were released soon after their arrest, "their indignation having been acknowledged to be legitimate." Obviously, the Romanian "Siguranta" did not always show such delicate courtesy.

6. *Korunk* was republished after 1957 under the direction Ernest Gáll, a member of the Romanian Academy. The review retained its pre-war layout and largely kept up its former quality.

7. The anti-Leninist dimension of Rosa Luxemburg's works was of particular interest to these milieus.

8. Published in Budapest in 1932, translated and annotated by Andor Lantos (the notes were actually written collectively). The text was discovered by Kautsky and published in 1903 in the review *Die Neue Zeit*. In France, Althusserians makes a big point of this, considering it to be a confirmation of their own "structuralist" interpretation of Marxism. The Budapest "notes" are intended to use Marx for a criticism of the Stalinist theory of the edification of socialism in one country. A new publication of the text in English — including the notes — would give rise to a fascinating debate.

9. Aladàr Mod, *Materialista Lételmélet* (Materialist Ontology) (Budapest, 1934).

# PART II

## Karl Mannheim

# 4

## Mannheim and the French Public:
## The Controversy over *Ideology and Utopia*

Karl Mannheim is a controversial scientific figure. Despite a partial French translation of *Ideologie und Utopie* published in 1956,[1] he met with limited success in French academia, where Lukàcs already had considerable influence even before the French translation of his magnum opus four years later. This difference in good fortune is not due to any difference in value or in level. Mannheim is the philosopher par excellence of times of crisis: misunderstood in peaceful periods, he is likely to be censored in periods of unrest. Adenauer's Germany could scarcely show enthusiasm for Mannheim; the Germany of Hitler (and of Honecker, as well) would not stand for him. A thinker trapped between the Scylla of disinterest and the Charybdis of censorship can hardly expect to have a steady readership. He may have had his hours of glory, however.

The publication of *Ideology and Utopia* in 1929 was one of them: it was a great event in the rich and tumultuous intellectual life of Weimar Germany. It caused debates among sociologists, political militants, and even theologians. Few books published at the time were such a faithful reflection of a thinker's intuitive reaction to the imminent rise of national socialism, which was more felt than understood;[2] few works responded so well to intellectual needs at a time when Europe, in the words of one commentator,[3] seemed weighed down under too much consciousness. "It is imperative," writes Mannheim,

in the present transitional period to make use of the intellectual twilight

33

which dominates our epoch and in which all values and points of view appear in their genuine relativity. We must realize once and for all that the meanings which make up our world are simply an historically determined and continuously developing structure in which man develops, and are in no sense absolute.

At this point in history when all things which concern man and the structure and elements of history itself are suddenly revealed to us in a new light, it behooves us in our scientific thinking to become masters of the situation, for it is not inconceivable that sooner than we suspect, as has often been the case before in history, this vision may disappear, the opportunity may be lost, and the world will once again present a static, uniform, and inflexible countenance.[4]

That is indeed what happened shortly after Mannheim's death. During the long period of economic expansion and political stabilization of postwar capitalism (the "glorious thirties"), the ideological crisis of the thirties was erased from the collective memory: in that climate, the works of thinkers like Mannheim were of interest only to specialists in the history of ideology. In periods of stabilization — the "organic periods" that Saint-Simon speaks of — the sociologist's task is not so much a dialectical study of truth integrated in historical becoming[5] as a quantitative and experimental analysis of social structures that are supposedly free from the servitudes of historicity.[6] Today, the situation has changed: for a few decades now, the Western world has entered a new period of questioning. After a long intellectual and social lull, Germany is once again becoming the ideological laboratory of Europe, as it was during the Weimar period, unfortunately, however, laboratories, even ideological ones, sometimes have a tendency to explode. In an article published in 1969 — a relatively calm time in comparison to the current situation — I called Mannheim "a philosophical storm bird;"[7] less than twenty years later, the storm is now *ante portas*. The new interest in Mannheim's thought is by no means a contingent phenomenon.

Mannheim was slow in arousing the interest of the French public. For a long time, he was overshadowed by Lukàcs, whose works, though similar in origin and comparable in level, benefited from the ardor and talent of Lucien Goldmann and excellent translators such as Maurice de Gandillac and Kostas Axelos. The French translation of *Ideology and Utopia*, on the other hand, was a passport to failure:

"The very rich oeuvre [of Mannheim], while it has stimulated sociological research on the social role of intellectuals and ideology, *has
not given rise to seminal influences.*"[8]

Some ink has been spilt over that translation. I believe that I was
the first one in France to point out some of its shortcomings.[9] P.J.
Simonds and D. Kettler seconded my criticisms in principle, but they
reproached me with failing to understand the degree to which
Mannheim, himself, was involved in the translation: the author, in full
agreement with the translators, wanted to make his work accessible to
a readership unacquainted with German philosophical terms.[10] According to Volker Meja, the English version "*is not a translation but
a substantially revised book.*"[11] That is precisely my opinion. But the
translators should have laid their cards on the table and presented
their work as a "new revised edition in collaboration with the author"
and not as "translated from the German." A translation should be
capable of being judged *as a translation,* and a translator should not
take advantage of the agreement of an author whose command of the
English language is dubious. A sociologist is perfectly entitled to
transpose his thought from the German philosophy of consciousness
(*Bewusstseinsphilosophie*) to Anglo-Saxon social psychology in light
of the specific receptivity of his new readership. He must not, however, translate "falsch ist ein theoretisches Bewusstsein" as "a theory
is therefore bad."[12] A thinker is the master of his thought; he is not the
master of the language.

These modifications were incorporated by the French translator,
who believed, in all good faith, that the English version was a *translation.* The situation justifying the modifications for Anglo-Saxon readers did not exist in France, which was just as steeped in philosophy as
Germany at the time. The changes in terminology that helped make
the book a success in the United States and England were no doubt
responsible for its failure in France. On the other hand, a faithful
translation based on the German original would have fit in perfectly
with the agitated intellectual climate of the declining Fourth Republic,
which had quite a bit in common with Weimar. At a time when the
issue of political alienation was in the forefront of French life (so
much so that it forced its way into the daily papers),[13] the message of
Mannheim, one of the major comtemporary theorists on that subject,
went practically unnoticed. The translation obscured Mannheim's most
modern side (as a demystifying thinker) and indirectly accentuated his

role as a sociologist of knowledge, in which he was most vulnerable to criticism. As a sociologist of knowledge he belonged to the intellectual universe of Weimar; as a demystifier, he belonged to Hungarian Marxism. When unburdened of the dead weight of the sociology of knowledge, Mannheim's works are rejuvenated to a remarkable extent. I shall try to reconstruct this "second face" of Mannheim in an attempt to answer some of the crucial questions of our times.

## Notes

1. The bibliography of Mannheim's works is not easy to draw up. Two collections of eassys published in English (Essays on the Sociology of knowledge, [London: Routledge & Kegan Paul, 1952] and Eassys on Sociology and Social Psychology [New York: Oxford University Press, 1953]) contain the translation of his main German-language essays. Those essays were reprinted after the war in the volume *Wissenssoziologie* (Berlin-Neuwied, Luchterhand Verlag, 1964). Consequently, some of Mannheim's works appear several times in the bibliography.

    The English translation of *Ideology and Utopia* (London: Routledge & Kegan, 1956) features a hitherto unpublished introduction written by Mannheim and an appendix taken from the *Handwörterbuch der Soziologie* by A. Vierkandt. That translation is crawling with errors. It is uncertain to what extent Mannheim is jointly responsible for those errors.

    The French translation by P. Rollet (Paris: Marcel Rivière, 1956) was based on the English translation and carries over its mistakes. I use it in quotations when it is faithful to the original; otherwise the translation is made directly from the fourth German printing (1965). References with no other indication refer to the latter text, whose pagination is considerably different from that of prewar editions. Finally, since the English translations are more accessible than the originals, I also give the English reference for important quotations.

2. I cannot resist the temptation to quote a truly prophetic passage of a novel published in 1928, shortly before *Ideology and Utopia*, very typical of the eschatological ambience of Germany at that time:

    A profound and morbid desire is manifest in the ranks of those who are moved by great problems. If nothing can be done (and I'm afraid it's already too late) then we must expect some fearful cataclysm that will outdo in terms of pure horror all the wars and revolutions we have seen up to now. Is it not strange that destruction stems from those who consider themselves to be the guardians of the most sacred values. (J. Wassermann, *L'Affaire Maurizius* [Paris: Plon 1930], 336).

3. R. Heiss, "Mannheim's Ideologie und Utopie," *Kölner Vierteljahrshefte für Soziologie, 1929,* 100.

4. Mannheim, *Ideologie and Utopie,* 76; English edition, 76.

5. Mannheim's expression: "In dem Werdestrom eingebettet," Ibid., 72.

6. With respect to the ideological role of quantitative sociology as an expression of an ahistorical (reified) perception of social reality, see Lucien Goldmann *Sciences humaines et philosophie* (Paris: P.U.F. 1953), 60.

7. In the review *L'Homme et la Société.* The same image is taken up in the excellent article by Rémy Hess, *Dictionnaire des Philosophes* (Paris: P.U.F. 1984), vol. II, 1736.

8. Unsigned article on Mannheim in the "Thesaurus" of the *Encyclopaedia Universalis.*

9. In my unpublished supplementary Ph.D. dissertation defended at the Sorbonne in Paris in 1962 and in the review *L'Homme et la Société* (January/March 1969): 130 ff.

10. "Although Gabel . . . makes appropriate and helpful observations about the translation, he does not seem to appreciate the extent of Mannheim's involvement in the enterprise." A.P. Simonds, *Karl Mannheim's Sociology of Knowledge* [Oxford: Clarendon Press, 1978], 16. Practically the same remark in D. Kettler, V. Meja, and N. Stehr: *Karl Mannheim,* (London and New York: Tavistock publ. 1984), 127.

11. Volker Meja, personal letter, December 1986.

12. *Ideologie und Utopie* (1965), 84; English edition (1948), 84. In the same passage "Falsch ist demnach im Ethischen ein Bewusstsein" is translated "an ethical attitude is invalid" (!). We have seen above that "utopisches Bewusstsein" is systematically translated "Utopian mentality." With or without Mannheim's consent, the whole demystifying message of this book is obscured by this translation.

13. I do not have the exact reference of the article of M. Duverger, "L'aliènation politique," published in *Le Monde* around 1959. The same author also speaks of "schizophrénie politique" (*Le Monde,* 14 February 1957 and *L'Express* of 13 February 1958), which amounts to the same thing.

# 5

# Ideology and False Consciousness

The problem of ideology and of false consciousness is in my view the central theme of Mannheim's thought. As a theorist of this problem, Mannheim remains a typical representative of the Hungarian marxist school ("Hungaro-Marxism") notwithstanding his later integration into German and Anglo-Saxon academic life. *Ideology and Utopia* is one of the rare Marxist works dedicated entirely to the problem of false consciousness. In that respect, despite some minor shortcomings, it merits a place in the history of ideas.

I shall try to show later on that Mannheim's much criticized theory of the rootless Intelligentsia cannot be understood outside the context of a general theory of false consciousness; otherwise it gives rise to all sorts of misinterpretations and misunderstandings. This same problem couched in borrowed terms occupies an important place in Mannheim's writings of the Anglo-saxon period of his career, in which he deliberately avoids using any terms with Marxist overtones.

The same holds true — though for different reasons — of some German texts of Mannheim, prior to *Ideology and Utopia*. In these texts the problem of false consciousness is implicitly present without being explicitly formulated. Mannheim's views, though virtually mature with respect to their substance, do not yet seem to have attained the fullness of their terminology. I shall analyze three of these essays, which might be called "masked" or indirect studies of false consciousness: a brochure on the interpretation of worldviews (*Weltanschauungs-Interpretation*), the essay on conservative ideology, and finally his article *Historismus*.[1]

The first of these studies is particularly interesting on account of its date of publication:[2] though published as a booklet in 1923, it first saw the light of day in 1921 as an article. As Mannheim's originality with respect to Lukàcs had been put in doubt (by Lucien Goldmann among others), it is important to note that its publication date is clearly prior to that of *History and Class Consciousness*. It outlines a project for interpreting cultural data in the light of "worldviews" (*Weltanschauung*) within the framework of a sociology of concrete dialectical totality.[3] The philosophical basis of this study by Mannheim is related to that of much more recent research into the sociology of literature by the late Lucien Goldmann.

Mannheim posits three levels of interpretation: objective, subjective, and documentary meanings (*Dokumentarsinn*). The concept of *documentary meaning* has been recently adopted by the ethnomethodical school of Garfinkel. According to Paul Kecskeméti, the latter two levels are analogous to the total and partial conceptions of ideology as elaborated in *Ideology and Utopia*.[4] Thus as early as 1921, Mannheim's works tackled the problem of false consciousness which, three years after the failure of the Hungarian Democratic Revolution of 1918, obsessed the protagonists of that drama, such as, among many others, Fogarasi and Paul Szende.

The problem is exemplified in a somewhat elementary manner by Mannheim. A man is going for a walk with a friend; they come across a beggar. The friend's act of charity can be interpreted according to three different criteria: as "objective" help to an unfortunate person, as an expression of a *conscious* charitable desire or, finally, as an *unconscious* manifestation of the desire to abreact his social guilt feelings. The quest for a hidden *Dokumentarsinn* is in this case evidently tantamount to unmasking a form of false consciousness.[5]

We should not overestimate the importance of this modest study which is certainly not comparable to the outstanding work of G. Lukàcs. Nonetheless the problems of quality and of intellectual priority are entirely different questions. According to Goldmann "the valid aspects of Mannheim's work had already appeared in *History and Class Consciousness*, which was his source of inspiration."[6] The date of publication of Mannheim's "modest study" is a clear warning against such superficial statements. Two years before the publication of the celebrated work by Lukàcs, it outlined the major themes and fundamental choices typical of Mannheim's period of maturity, such as the importance of the problem of ideology, the primacy of the concept of *Weltanschauung*, some indifference to the problem of materialism in philosophy, and an overall dialectical orientation. It appears that from the very outset of his career as a thinker, the future "bourgeois Marxist" takes the diametrically opposite turn to what was to become the "official Marxism" of the Stalinist era.

Mannheim's essay on the ideology of German conservatism (*Das Konservative Denken*) is his best work according to Raymond Aron and the most disconcerting one for a Marxist reader.[7] The imperviousness of conservative political thought to all aspects of the dialectic — including its historicist facet — has always been an article of faith for the Marxist vulgate. Mannheim's essay shows that the worldview of German conservatism implies some genuine dialectical elements as a defensive reaction against the reified rationalism of the bourgeoisie: life opposed to concepts, a taste for individualism and for historicism. Seen in the light of Mannheim's exegesis, the ideology of German conservatism appears as diametrically opposed to that of racist ethnocentricity, which is based on a reified and impersonalizing vision of the discriminated outgroup (Adorno).

The reader is naturally entitled to pose the question, what has that essay to do with the problem of false consciousness? Here I see an indirect but significant relationship. It is a well-known historical fact that Hitlerism rose to power in alliance with the conservative political forces of Weimar Germany. For many German and foreign observers, whether for or against nazism, this conservative alliance legitimated a sort of identity; by discarding democracy and turning to Hitler, Germany was supposed to have "rediscovered its atemporal essence."[8] In this perspective the myth of the "eternal Germany," tantamount to an antihistoricist (reified ) vision of the "German problem," is a manifestation of false consciousness which contributed to occulting the historical specificity of the Hitlerian phenomenon as a form of "after-capitalism" (Burnham) and thus helped to create a climate favorable to "collaboration" in certain conservative milieus of the occupied countries. By pointing out basic differences between the *Weltanschauung* of the German conservatives and that of the Hitlerites, Mannheim contributed an important argument to this crucial debate.

His historicist commitment is meaningful only as a reaction against the antihistoricism of the ideological discourse. The historicity of social data is an obvious fact; it is the ideological negation of this evidence that justifies historicism as a school. Rather than a theory, historicism is a counter-ideology.[9] This aspect of the question has been overlooked by critics who judge the historicist school out of its ideological context. The expression "false consciousness" is not even used once in K. Popper's book, which is intended to be a final refutation of historicism.[10] Moreover, Popper seems to have started out with an arbitrary defintion. He assumes that the historicist hypothesis of *the possibility of historical forecasts* is the essence of their credo;[11] that definition, however, certainly has nothing in common with the one Mannheim used. In my view, the two essential ideas of Mannheim's historicism are the historical validity of the category of totality[12] and a view that he probably borrowed from Dilthey, i.e. that there are no absolutes outside history; historicism is the heir to metaphysics.[13] Thus, historicism appears as the negation of biological idols incarnating the reified, antihistorical essence of racist false consciousness.

Mannheim appears in this light, along with Lukàcs, Szende, and a few other less important figures, as one of the rightful heirs to this tumultuous chapter of Marxist doctrine which is the critical analysis of the ideological discourse (*Ideologiekritik*). He has often been censured for the supposed indecision in his use of concepts. In my view, that indecision reflected the confusion present in texts written by Marx and Engels themselves, which went unnoticed because of the authority granted to these works even in the camp of their opponents. Mannheim's main scientific ambition, when elaborating his theory, was obviously to provide a conceptual clarification that lead to an unbiased theory of political alienation.

This attempt at conceptual clarification functions in two principal directions. Mannheim tries to find a common denominator between the concept of ideology and utopia, and at the same time he aims to define and differentiate the Marxist concept of ideology. These two attempts are of unequal pertinence. Mannheim failed in his search for a common denominator of the concepts of ideology and utopia, largely because of the ambiguity, and the slightly metaphysical overtone, of the term *Seinstranszendenz* (transcendent with regard to the social reality). On the other hand, Mannheim's distinction between the various "conceptions" of ideology is, in my view, an entirely original and valid contribution to this important problem.

Three types of split come into play in Mannheim's exploration of the ideological phenomenon: the "evaluative" versus the "nonevaluative" conception of ideology;[14] the "particular" versus its "total" conception, and finally the "special" versus the "general" one. The first of these oppositions requires no explanation. The "particular" conception of ideology implies that the opponent's ideas "are regarded as more or less conscious disguises of the real nature of a situation" (*Ideology and Utopia*, 1948, 49). For the "total" conception the ideological distortion is an *effet de perspective*, i.e. a consequence of a socially determined, neo-structuration of the logical framework of political consciousness.[15] This neo-structuration may in a sectarian and egocentric political context result in the emergence of acute forms of false consciousness such as Stalinism characterized, as is well known, by its propensity for ex post facto reevaluation of historical facticities (Orwell) and by the parasitary preponderance of identificatory function in the field of logic ("hitléro-trotskism"; "social-fascism" etc).[16]

As for the distinction between the "special" and "general" conceptions of ideology, it is of a different order. The special conception of ideology is the expression of a polemical point of view in which the proper ideology occupies a privileged place and, in fact, is no longer branded as an ideology in the Marxist (pejorative) sense of the term. The general conception of ideology "is being used by the analyst when he has the courage to subject not just the adversary's point of view but all points of view, including his own, to the ideological analysis" (Mannheim *Ideology and Utopia*, 69). The special conception of ideology legitimates the egocentric-manichean trend of committed political thought, while its general conception implies a criticism of this tendency. Moreover it puts the emphasis on the importance of *structural changes* in the logical framework of political consciousness while the deliberate mystification (political falsehood) is, on the contrary, the central category of the special conception.

Mannheim's ambition was to move from politics to social science whilst continuing to apply the techniques of debunking used in political debate. The "scientific politics" which is supposed to result from this approach is called upon as an ideological guide for the "democratic planning" that is the central leitmotif of his writings in his Anglo-Saxon period. The role of the rootless Intelligentsia takes concrete shape. Mannheim does not refer to academic scholarship but to the objectivity of an "ideal-typical" unattached intellectual, capable of transcending the various forms of social egocentricity such as ethnocentrism, eurocentrism, or class-related egocentricity, thanks to his ability to move within different historical perspectives.

One might wonder whether this differentiation corresponds to a genuine necessity or whether it is symptomatic of Mannheim's excessive taste for nuances. In practice the "particular," "partial," and "evaluative" conceptions of ideology amount to the same thing. Blaming an opponent for deliberate mystification implies that the accuser is in the right and that his point of view therefore represents a "superior value." Similarly the distinction between the "total," "general," and "nonevaluative" conceptions of ideology becomes blurred in practice; if you consider the opponent's political consciousness to be "socially determined," it is difficult to deny that your own consciousness is determined in a similar matter, unless you admit that the latter is extra-social, i.e. in fact *utopian*. A bipolar typology suffices in practice: a polemical conception of ideology as a corollary of political falsehood, versus a structural one as corollary of false consciousness. At any rate, this Mannheimian surgery might restore a minimum of health to the concept of ideology branded by the outstanding French theorist of Marxism, G. Labica, as a "sick concept."[17] It is regrettable that — like Marx and Engels — Mannheim did not investigate thoroughly the problem of the relationship between ideology and false consciousness. The exact nature of the ideological distortion is not defined in *Ideology and Utopia,* and we find no attempt in this work to explain the origin and the psycho-sociological mechanism (the "pathogeny") of this distortion.[18] Mannheim prefers examples to definitions; he seems to have an intuitive notion rather than a clear idea of false consciousness. The difference between ideology and false consciousness is so hazy that one wonders whether the author of *Ideology and Utopia* does not use the terms synonymously.[19]

According to Mannheim a form of moral consciousness is false "if it is oriented with reference to norms, with which action in a given historical setting, even with the best of intentions, cannot comply." There is false consciousness in the theoretical field when "in a given practical situation it uses concepts and categories which, if taken seriously, would prevent man from adjusting himself at that historical stage."[20] It appears that in Mannheim's view, false consciousness is first and foremost history-blindness and society-blindness. These views are highly akin to those of young Marx.

A short literary digression may illustrate this interpretation. An immortal model of the ideologist is found in literature: Don Quixote. The genius of Cervantez was successful in combining, within a single character, the nobility of idealists, the "history-blindness" of ideologists, and the schizophrenic side of false consciousness. That subject deserves to be studied in its own right. I shall simply mention the leptosomatic nature of Don Quixote. The duo Don Quixote, Sancho Panza prefigures the characterology of Kretschmer (Leptosomatic / schizoid versus pyknic / cycloid). Identification also plays a large role in schizophrenia. Géza Róheim speaks of an "identification with the past" among schizophrenics.[21] Psychoanalysts (such as Clara Thomson) have used the term "alienating identification." The Italo-American psychiatrist Silvano Arieti has pointed out the role of identification in *the logic* of schizophrenics.[22]

This "alienating identification with the past," which is an important factor in schizophrenia, also dominates most of Don Quixote's actions during his insanity. "And Sancho, don't think I am swearing this oath lightly, for *I am following a model*: the same thing happened to Sacripan, word for word, with the helmet of Mambrin."[23] This type of reasoning is a leitmotif in Don Quixote, popping up at every turn in the novel.

Don Quixote's visual illusions are genuine delusional perceptions (*Wahnwahrnehmungen*) admirably described as such by Cervantes. Psychopathologists generally agree in considering optical hallucinations to be symptomatic of schizophrenia. In his *Theorie des Romans*, Lukàcs observes a "demonical narrowing of the soul" in Don Quixote;[24] for a psychopathologist this is very clearly reminiscent of schizophrenic autism. A Hungarian psychoanalyst Léopold Szondi — author of the well-known projective test that bears his name — spoke of "systole of the Ego," and Don Quixote's personality is a fine illustration (I don't dare speak of proof) of the schizophrenic structure of false consciousness.

After this literary digression, let us return to the ticklish problem that was Mannheim's stumbling block: the relationship between ideology and false consciousness. While the implied definition of false consciousness underlying the above examples is based on the criterion of dephasing, Mannheim's definition of ideology is founded on transcendence of social being (*Seinstranszendenz*). Mannheim tried to use this concept as a bridge between ideology and utopia; he claimed that ideology was a conservative form of that type of "transcendence," whereas utopia was its revolutionary (*seinssprengend*) form.

I will examine the difficulties of that synthesis later. I shall now clarify a problem of translation that is largely responsible for numerous misinterpretations of Mannheim. In the English translation of *Ideology and Utopia*, "*Seinstranszendent*" became "situationally transcendent" (*Ideology and Utopia*, 175 ff.); this is a genuine mistranslation. It seems more advisable to conserve the original German term in quotation marks with a translator's note. I shall sometimes resort to this technique, since anything is better than establishing a chronic misinterpretation of a thinker's work.

The problem of the relationship between ideology and false consciousness is certainly raised by Mannheim but not resolved. In his view the application of Christian principles by a society that turned its back on them is an ideological attitude.[25] That may be true; however given the fact that this last example corresponds to the above-mentioned illustrations of false consciousness, the difference between ideology and false consciousness is unclear. Moreover, there is nothing imaginary about Mannheim's example. In the America of "Uncle Tom's Cabin," admirable Quakers helped fugitive slaves across the Canadian border. Their moral consciousness was certainly "*seinstranszedent,*" as is any moral consciousness worthy of the name. Nonetheless, one could scarcely call them ideologists or utopians. The conservative or mystifying role of their "ideology" is not obvious. John Brown was a martyr for the ideal of equality, but he was neither an ideologist nor a utopian.

Ethnocentric ideologies, however, are genuine ideologies with an obvious mystifying function; they do not merit being called "seinstranszedent." Their anti-dialectical, dichotomizing, reifying, and depreciating conception of the allegedly "inferior" race is *transcended by the social reality*, and not vice versa. The same holds true for all forms of political Manichaeism characterized by a simplistic view of the enemy. They are ideologies or at least forms of false of consciousness; there is nothing "transcendental" about them in the philosophical, or even the ordinary sense of the term.

Another of Mannheim's examples, which is also quoted in a recent book by Raymond Boudon, concerns "the taboo against taking interest on loans."[26] Such a taboo was legitimate in a "society based upon intimate and neighbourly relations"; it becomes outmoded (ideological) in a capitalist context (*Ideology and Utopia,* 1948, 85). The concept of "transcendence with regard of the social reality" (*Seinstranszendenz*) sheds no light on this subject. The paradoxical survival of this taboo was, according to Mannheim, due to the legal structure's failing to keep in step with the evolution of the economic infrastructure; it appears in this light as a phenomenon of "society-blindness" and "history-blindness." One remembers here the classical statement of young Marx: Ideology is tantamount to negation or distortion of historical data.

The same holds true for racist consciousness, which appears as a form of false consciousness since it reifies ethnic attributes instead of functionalizing them from a socio-historical point of view. A form of political consciousness is false when in the presence of two competing systems it judges one according to ethical norms and the other with respect to the principles of the *raison d'état.*[27] The tendency to arbitrary identification of different—and sometimes hostile—elements of the political outgroup is one of the typical features of the logic of political alienation.[28] Finally a political consciousness is false when it attributes the responsibility for a historically fatal change to the clandestine action of evil external forces. By extending this last notion, false consciousness may be defined in a general manner as *"heteronymic consciousness."* Due to his lack of a precise definition (*"per falsam conscientam intelligo id"*), Mannheim neither succeeds in drawing the boundary line between false consciousness and ideology nor in encompassing the concrete richness of both of those concepts.

This lack has not gone unnoticed. We are familiar with the type of overzealous translator eager to make up for the author's failings: unfortunately, not all of them are up to the job. The English and French translations include a "definition" of false consciousness: "Fausse gonscience, c'est-à-dire *l'esprit complètement déformé* qui falsifie tout ce qui vient à sa portée" (False consciousness . . . that is the completely distorted mind which falsifies everything that comes within its range).[29] This definition *is not featured in the original German.* It is therefore an interpolation made either by Mannheim or—more likely—by the translators. It is unacceptable for several reasons. Translating *"Bewusstsein"* (consciousness) as "mind" (or "esprit") already suggests a dangerous intellectualization of the problem of consciousness in general and false consciousness in particular. The absence of a veritable definition of the Marxist notion of "consciousness," which is often used in practice as synonymous with "knowledge" or even "thought," paved the way for a theoretical interpretation that, when carried to its logical conclusion, threatens to reduce to a banality all the theory of false consciousness.

But above all, the expression "which falsifies everything" is highly misleading for an uninformed reader.[30] False consciousness is not due to inaccuracy but to the lack of sociological functionalization. In this regard, the problem that it poses is related to that of the dialectical totality. It is not a "completely perverted mind that falsifies everything" but a form of consciousness incapable of incorporating into concrete socio-historical structures facts that are likely to be accurate *in isolation.* A century ago, a Confederate American who believed that the intellectual level of the recently emancipated slaves was not, on the average, on a par with whites, would not be making, in principle, an "inaccurate" observation. Nonetheless, his opinion would be ideological (symptomatic of false consciousness) if he were to reify ("naturalize") such transitory inferiority as the expression of natural or divine law ("the curse of Ham") instead of recognizing it as a historically rooted social fact. The basic category of ideologization is not inaccuracy, as Raymond Boudon, Parsons, and Lucien Goldmann before them would have it, but the lack of functional analysis from a historical and sociological point of view. It is not due to inaccurate thinking but to a "sub-dialectical," ahistorical viewpoint.

From the very start, the theory of ideology was torn between a "cognitivo-Manichean" conception, which considers the essence of the debate to be the opposition between accuracy and inaccuracy (i.e., truth and falsehood) and a dialectical-historicist conception which puts emphasis on the socially determined, logical restructuralizing, without focusing on questions of accuracy and inaccuracy, which it leaves to epistemologists. Boudon places Marx in the first category, which seems somewhat arbitrary.[31] In "The German Ideology," the notion of ideology is defined in strictly historicist terms as the result of a distortion or abstraction of history."[32] In the "Peasant War in Germany" Engels is ironical about "German Ideology that still sees the struggles of the Middle Ages as violent theological arguments" and 1789 as a somewhat animated discussion about the advantages of constitutional monarchy over an absolute one.[33] The criticism of the "founding fathers" of the Marxist theory was that ideologists lacked a functional socio-historical analysis; to be brief, they blamed ideologists for fragmenting the dialectical totality that forms the superstructures with the infrastructures. The opposite point of view can also find substance in genuine Marxian texts; one cannot ask of Marxism, which is at the same time a critique of ideologies and also an ideology itself, the coherence provided by Durkheim's school, for example.[34]

The late Lucien Goldmann, who was a serious scholar of Marxism and a strict orthodox Marxist, also opted for a "cognitive" interpretation. He had studied the problem of false consciousness, but this was a secondary aspect of his work: he was first and foremost a sociologist of literature. In his conferences at the international Congress of Sociology in Stresa (1959) and at a Royaumont seminar (1960)[35] he underlined the importance of the concept of "inadequacy" for the definition of false consciousness, which would be in this perspective a system of inadequacies (errors) of social origin, that is to say, linked or related to social being (*Seinsverbunden*). This interpretation incorporates too many different types of inadequacies "linked to social being," which prevents an overall description of this phenomenon and renders difficult the elaboration of its global theory. Another problem is that genuine forms of false consciousness may be overlooked. The illusion of a Russian noble living in Paris just after October 1917, who expects the "inevitable" breakdown of the Soviet government, is most certainly an "inadequacy linked to his class situation," but such an illusion could not be incorporated into a consistent theory of false consciousness. On the other hand, Hitlerite ideology, an expression of a genuine form of false consciousness, was far more than a mere system of errors; it involved a delirious dimension as do all other forms of racism. The perception of the social world corollary of false consciousnes is not inadequate, but to use Bleuler's term "dereistic"; the two terms are not synonyms. The difference between these two terms is the same as that which at the individual level distinguishes error from psychiatric delusion.[36] Goldmann's "cognitive" approach (as well as that of Talcott Parsons) ignores the dereistic dimension of the ideological discourse which is essential;  it thus propels this investigation towards an impasse.[37]

The same holds true for the definition suggested by M. Raymond Boudon, who defines ideology as "a doctrine based on a scientific theory and equipped with excessive or unfounded credibility."[38] I wonder what criteria would define the degree of *legitimate credibility* of a doctrine? According to Professor Boudon's definition, if Germany had won the last war, Hitler's triumphant racism would cease to be an ideology, as its "credibility" would have been legitimized, so to speak, by military victory. Do pacifist and "Green" movements of European countries have an ideological aspect? Boudon's definition, paralyzed, as it were, by "cognitve prejudice," offers hardly any answers to these important questions.[39]

There is some confusion in the debate on the problem of ideology. The typology suggested by Mannheim in *Ideology and Utopia* offers a good arm for eliminating such confusion. The "polemical" conception of ideology, which covers inaccuracies due to ignorance or mystification, must be differentiated from its structural conception, which incorporates socially determined distortions that frequently concern the logical structure of the discourse. We are here faced with the main stumbling block of the theory of ideology — the secret of the paradoxical credibility of sometimes absurd ideas in politics,[40] the mystery of false consciousness in short. That mystery has inspired innumerable explanatory theories that are generally disappointing. Orthodox Marxism stresses the importance of "class interest," but it overlooks the difference between interest and "genuine interest," i. e. between "short-term interest" and "long-term interest." Moreover the "theory of class interest" proves a failure with respect to an important ideological phenomenon of the postwar period as the blind spot of intellectual "fellow travellers," such as Jean-Paul Sartre, vis-à-vis Stalinism.[41] The factor "passion" is of poor explanatory value. Passion may be either a cause or an effect; it may also be absent.[42] As for the theory of Geertz, it has no explanatory ambitions as such.[43]

The historicist and dialectical criterion of ideologization, on the other hand, has a genuine explanatory aspect. It was not systematically explored by Mannheim; nonetheless it is located in the straight line of his general approach to the problem. An historicist and dialectical understanding of social reality — the social awareness according to Mannheim's terminology — is a difficult mental technique that is the outcome of a process of maturation: man is not born a dialectician and historicist, *he becomes one*. The man in the street cares little about the historical aspect of problems; his consciousness is centered on the present and for this reason falls frequently into the trap of ideologization. The same holds true *a fortiori* for a man in the crowd.[44] The media contribute to ideologization by depenalizing illiteracy and by divorcing the present from its historical roots. Old newspapers can be filed or looked up in a public library, but few people are in position to file television news. Orwell saw clearly the importance of television as a possible instrument of totalitarian rape of public opinions (the telescreen in *1984*). Thinking of the present "historically" requires a certain degree of intellectual maturity and effort. One of the main attractions of ideology is its anti-historicist and anti-dialectical character; it offers an *economie d'effort* to lazy minds. The favorable reception by intellectually developed milieus of typical anti-historicist and anti-dialectical ideologies such as racism and Stalinism is a case in point.

The notion of "inaccuracy" is a corollary of the polemical conception of ideology that plays a major role in the viewpoints of authors like L. Goldmann and T. Parsons (and, to a certain extent, R. Boudon). That notion is certainly valid in the area of epistemology but is rather risky in political sociology, since it lends itself to arbitrary sociocentric use. There is a danger that the "correct theory" will be defined as the one approved by university authorities, in the best of cases, and by political authorities, in the worst. It is no coincidence that the authoritarian mind leans toward the partial and particular (polemical) conception of ideology ("our enemies are liars or ignoramuses"), whereas the total and general (structural) conception of ideology is the natural corollary of a democratic, pluralist view. Mannheim's theory of ideology — as do all of his works — contains the elements of a plea for democracy. Taking into consideration the political situation of today's world, that is certainly one of its merits.

## Notes

1. In *Archiv für Sozialwissenchaft und Sozialpolitik*, 1924, tome 52, reprinted in *Wissenssoziologie* Berlin-Neuwied, Luchterland Verl. 1964, 246–307. In English in *Essays on the Sociology of Knowledge* (London: Routledge et Kegan, 1952).
2. Mannheim, *Beiträge zur Theorie der Weltanschauungs — Interpretation, Jahrbuch für Kunstgeschichte* 1921–1922, reprinted in *Wissenssoziologie*, 91–154. In English in: *Essays on the Sociology of Knowledge*, 33–83.
3. Das neuauftretende geschichtsphilosophische Interesse das sich von Seiten des Spezialforschers dadurch verrät, dass er ein wachsendes Bedürfnis hat, seine Spezialergebnisse in der Totalität des gesamten historischen Prozesses zu verankern (Mannheim, *Beiträge zur Theorie des Weltan-*

*schauungs-Interpretation*, 9, *Wissenssoziologie*, 96). Cf. English translation: "This interest manifests itself by a growing need to fit particular
findings into some global historical schema" (*Essays on the Sociology of
Knowledge* [London: Routledge & Kegan Paul, 1952], 37). This translation is not bad, but it does not fully render the dialectical character of
Mannheim's way of proceeding; the German term *Totalität* is infinitely
more meaningful than *global historical schema*.

4. "Yet the concept of documentary meaning transcends pure
*Geistesgeschichte*. It is an existential concept: it is first introduced in
connection with the problem of unconscious hypocrisy, of a false consciousness or not 'genuine' (*uneigentlich*) existence as the existentialists
would put it. This foreshadows the concept of 'total ideology,' one of the
most provocative ideas in *'Ideology and Utopia'* " (Paul Kecskeméti,
Préface to *Essays on the Sociology of Knowledge*, 13).

5. *Beiträge zur Theorie der Weltanschauung-Interpretation*, p. 15: English
translation 45.

6. Lucien Goldmann, *Sciences humaines et philosophie* (Paris: P.U.F, 1952),
39. This all-too-harsh criticism in the well-known book by L. Goldmann
has certainly helped to discredit temporarily Mannheim's work in France.

7. Karl Mannheim, *Das Konservative Denken* (Soziologische Beiträge zum
Werden des Politisch-historischen Denkens in Deutschland, *Archiv für
Sozialwissenschaft und Sozialpolitik*, 1927), t. 57, reprinted in *Wis-
senssoziologie*, 408-508 . English translation in *Essays on Sociology and
Social Psychology* (New York: Oxford University Press, 1953), 74-164.
As for Aron's favorable appreciation, see Raymond Aron, *La sociologie
allemande contemporaine* (Paris: P.U.F, 1935), 86.

8. "Hindenburg hoped that Hitler might bring Germany round again to the
ideas of order and authority which were current in his youth. He might
end up by re-establishing the monarchy." A. Fabre-Luce, *Histoire de le
Révolution européenne* (Paris, Domat, 1954), 104.

9. The historical nature of individual existence is obvious to all but the
insane or neurotic; the psychoanalytic cure of schizophrenia often con-
sists in a technique of *individual historicizing*. See the works of the psychoanalyst Gisèle Pankow summarized in Gabel: *False Consciousness*
(New York: Harper & Row, 1978), 228–29.

10. K. Popper, *Misère de l'historicisme* (Paris: Plon, 1956).

11. Certain ideologies have a strong leaning towards historical predictions
although they are diametrically opposed to genuine historicism. The most
typical example is undoubtedly Stalinism, with its tendency towards an
analogical intepretation of history ("The Western powers *continue* Hitler's
war"), which is of course incompatible with the historical validity of the
totality, as bearer of the specificity of historical data.

There is some confusion about the definition of the concept of historicism. I have often suggested differenciating prospective historicism ("History has a meaning") from retrospective historicism ("the historical dimension of facts is the key to their essence") and using the dualism of French terminology ("l'historisme" and "historicisme") to emphasize the ambiguity of the concept. According to Boudon, *"l'historisme* ne doit pas être confondu avec *l'historicisme,"* (in Popper's sense, search for the laws of history) which is the opposite (Raymond Boudon, *L'idéologie* [Paris: Fayard, 1986], 300).

12. "Historicism has nothing in common with a mechanical summing up of isolated results concerning historical science. . . . It aspires to the status of a genuine philosophy, capable of going beyond the beginnings of epistemology and serving as a basis for the latter. Its place is much the same as that formerly occupied by metaphysics. . . . Its procedure is intended to transcend isolated historical facts and to look for the profound unity of historical becoming by *using the category of the totality."* This quotation comes from an article of Mannheim: "Historismus," published in the German monthly *Archiv für Sozialwissenschaft und Sozialpolitik* [1924]: 53 ff. It was republished later on in the volume *Wissenssoziologie* [Berlin-Neuwied: Luchterhand Verlag: 1964], 246–307. There is an English translation in the volume *Essays on the Sociology of Knowledge* [London: Routledge & Paul Kegan, 1952], 33–58.)

   Cf, Merleau-Ponty: "Being a Marxist . . . means thinking . . . that history is Gestalt in the sense that Gerrnan authors give this word: a total process moving towards a state of equilibrium: a classless society. (*Humanisme et Terreur* [Paris: Gallimard, 1947], 127).

   Whether Louis Althusser is in agreement or not, Marxism is indeed a type of historicism and Mannheim is a bourgeois Marxist.

13. "Historical consciousness is not only the living refutation of metaphysics, it is moreover its inheritor." Raymond Aron, *Essai sur la théorie de l'histoire dans l'Allemagne contemporaine* (Paris: Vrin, 1936), 30.

14. Obviously, translating *Wertfrei* as "non-evaluative" and *Wertend* as "evaluative" is to be taken with precaution, but it is hard to find the perfect translation.

15. Mannheim uses both "*seinsgebunden*" and "*seinsverbunden.*" There is a nuance of difference between these two terms, since the prefix "*ver*" is often pejorative in German. This calls to mind the distinction made by some English-speaking authors between the social *determination* and *origin* of thought. In regard to the translation, we can choose between "pensée rapportée au plan social" (R. Aron), which is more precise, and "pensee liée à l'être," which is less unwieldy. I have thus opted for the second.

16. This is typically the case of the logic underlying Stalinist ideology: logic of identification ("Hitlero-Trotskyism") arising from the illegitimate "ontologization" (reification) of a partial historical perspective.

17. G. Labica, "Pour une approche critique du concept d'idéologie," *Tiers-Monde* 15 (1974): 31 (A critical approach to the concept of ideology).

18. In a certain number of publications directly influenced by Mannheim, I have tried to characterize the structural transformation of the logic underlying the ideologization process as basically being an anti-dialectical process arising from collective egocentricity (sociocentricity, ethnocentricity, Eurocentricity, etc.) and capable of leading, in the extreme form, to logical structures similar to those characteristic of schizophrenia. For details see Gabel *False Consciousness* (New York: Harper & Row, 1978), 78 ff ("Schizophrenic structure of ideological throught; Political alienation").

19. It is difficult to draw the precise boundaries of false consciousness and ideology, since there are so many transitional forms. The behavior of a man who is theoretically opposed to racism but who frowns upon his daughter's intentions to marry a black, is halfway between false consciousness and ideology; it is a little more than false consciousness, but a little less than concretized ideology. The best analogy comes from psychopathology: false consciousness corresponds to the diffuse state of delirium (the *Wahnstimmung* of German authors) and ideology to concretized delirium.

20. *Ideologie und Utopie* (1965), 83–4. English edition, 84.

21. G. Roheim, *Magic and Schizophrenia* (New York: International Universites Press, 1955), 35.

22. Silvano Arieti, *Interpretation of Schizophrenia* (New York: Basic Books, 1974), 232.

23. Cervantes, *Don Quichotte* (Toulouse, Privat), 2nd part, vol. 1, 102.

24. "Dämonische Verengerung der Seele" G. Lukàcs, *Die Theorie des Romans, Ein geschichtsphilosophischer Versuch über die Formen der grossen Epik* (Berlin: Cassirer Verlag, 1920), 95. The Hungarian psychoanalyst Léopold Szondi spoke in the same way of the "systole of the Ego" (Egosystole).

25. Mannheim, *Ideologie und Utopie,* German edition, 171. English edition, 175.

26. R. Boudon, *L'idéologie,* 70.

27. Here I am referring to the judgements made in certain circles concerning the politics of Israel and its enemies. The surprise attack on Yom Kippur in 1973 was justified by the *raison d'Etat*; the Israeli attack on the nuclear power plant in Tammouz is branded as being contrary to the international moral principles.

28. Quite recently, an Iranian government spokesman accused Bagdad of being a "Zionist government"! (See *Le Figaro*, Paris, 25 July 1983).
29. *Ideology and Utopia*, English translation, 62. The definition in question ought to be on p. 64 of the latest German edition (1965); but it is not to be found there, as is the case in all the prewar editions.
30. Even insane thinking does not "falsify everything in its reach"; a paranoiac may be an excellent physicist.
31. Boudon, *L'idéologie*, 37.
32. Marx, *Die Deutsche Ideologie*, Berlin 1932, Abt.I.t.5. p.568. This passage is one of the "Textvarianten" of the German original, which does not make it any less important.
33. F. Engel, *La Guerre des Paysans en Allemagne* (Paris: Editions Sociales, 1974), 61.
34. For more information about the "dualism" of Marxist doctrine, see the enlightening article by Maxime Rodinson, "Sociologie marxiste et idéologie marxiste," *Diogéne*, octobre-décembre 1960.
35. L. Goldmann, *"Potential Consciousness and False Consciousness,"* The World Congress on Sociology, Stresa, 1958, and *"Potential Consciousness,"* The Congress on Communication, Royaumont, 1960.
36. The difference between *error* ("inaccurate" understanding) and *delusion* ("unrealistic" understanding) is well-established in psychopathology. This distinction is useful for the studies of ideology. A fictitious example illustrates the difference between "inaccurate" and "unrealistic" understanding. Imagine two neighbors: a foreign military attaché and a peaceable craftsman. Their phone lines are dependent on the same exchange, which is not working properly. They both come up with the same false explanation: wire tapping. They make the same mistake, *but it is not really the same mistake*. In fact, the social status of the military attaché implies that it is possible (or even probable) that his line is tapped, so his error is rather banal: he simply made an inaccurate choice from among the comparable legitimate possibilities. The apparently identical mistake of his neighbor, on the other hand, may be the prodrome of incipient psychosis. Thus, it is an "error" that is much more than an error.

The second type of "error" is typical of false consciousness. The illusions of Communist "fellow travellers" who perceived Stalin as the benevolent "father of the people" for decades, the illusions of intellectuals such as Michel Foucault who welcomed in Khomeini's revolution as a breath of fresh air, are not due to intellectual weakness, ignorance, or bad faith, but to a Manichean (anti-dialectical) polarization of their political universe; anything anti-American is automatically supposed to be good.

A good many well-informed Frenchmen believed in good faith in

Vichy France that the Jews were responsible for triggering off the Second World War. That war broke out between two antisemitic states in which the Jewish minority had no influence and "world Judaism," which was supposedly omnipotent, did not even have enough power at the time to obtain sanctuary for its countless refugees without a country. The question of the responsibility of the Jews in starting the war is a typical ideological theme, but it goes far beyond simple "inaccuracy"; it is a delusional type of "unrealistic" construction. For more on this question, see Léon Poliakov, *La Causalité diabolique* (Paris: Calmann-Lévy, 1982), who, without using the term, offers an excellent critical analysis of one aspect of false consciousness.

37. Talcott Parsons quoted by Boudon, *L'ideologie*, 35.
38. Ibid., 52.
39. The above-suggested criterion of heteronomy provides an answer to some of these questions. Pacifist and ecological movements are ideological to the extent that their secret objective is not to maintain peace or conserve the environment but to upset the political and economic balance to the benefit of certain powers. Thus, it goes without saying that political consciousness of militants in such movements is a type of false consciousness. There is still a problem: how is it possible to show the "secret" motivations of the supporters of such groups? God alone is considered capable of knowing our intimate thoughts, but the obvious partiality of certain political judgements and actions provides sufficient proof. The pacifism of those who condemned Margaret Thatcher in 1982 while showing understanding for General Galtieri and the anti-nuclear policy of the movements based exclusively on criticizing western countries are undeniably ideological in nature.
40. Boudon, *L'ideologie*, 92.
41. The case of the "fellow travellers" is a good illustration of the ahistorical, anti-dialectical character of ideology. The expression "the enemies of my enemies are my friends" is of one of the key formulas providing access to the world of the fellow travellers (David Caute, *Les compagnons de route* [Paris: Robert Laffont, 1979], 291). The political consciousness of fellow travellers is characterized by its Manicheism and by its anti-dialectical opposition between appearance and essence, or, if you prefer, between "phenomenon" and "noumenon" (political Kantianism). The "Stalinist Russia" phenomenon may well be abhorrent, but its suprahistorical "noumenon" is still progressivist in the eyes of the fellow traveller.
42. Boudon, *L'idéologie*, 76.
43. Boudon, (Ibid., 36) relates a discussion between Sutton and Geertz's about a unionist text calling the anti-unionist Taft-Hartley Law a "slave

labor law." According to Sutton it is a distortion; in Geertz's view, it was nothing but a metaphor. In fact, it was a discreet form of the customary paralogism of leftist and rightist totalitarian ideologies, i.e *false identification*. Many perfectly well-meaning, brilliant intellectuals seriously believe that Israel is a fascist state (see, among others, the assertions of Bruno Kreisky in *France Soir*, 16 June 1982) and Trotsky an agent sponsored by Nazi Germany. Those are not metaphors but manifestations of sociocentric, sub-dialectical logic. By refusing to consider ideology to be consubstantial with distortion, Geertz gets rid of the problem of false consciousness and avoids having to give an explanatory theory; the use of metaphors is a natural penchant of political discourse requiring no special explanation.

44. A large fraction of progressivist and third-world opinion considers Israel to be a colonialist phenomenon: it forgets that Israel's existence as a state originated in a strictly classical, anticolonialist revolt. There is no end to the list of such examples of social amnesia aggravated by the media, which isolate current events from their historical context.

# 6

# The Problem of the
# "Socially Unattached Intelligentsia"

> ... angeli che non furon ribelli né fur fedeli a
> Dio, ma per sé foro.
> — Dante, *Inferno*

> Anyone who by nature and not by circum-
> stance, chose to exist without a country would
> be a detestable character, far above or below
> other men
> — Aristotle, *Politics*

Mannheim's theory of the "socially unattached Intelligentsia" (*freischwebende Intelligenz*) is without doubt the most criticized and misunderstood theory in all of his works. The fact that the passages in
*Ideology and Utopia* dealing with that issue were arbitrarily omitted
from the French translation left it even more open to misinterpretation.

Goldmann claimed that Mannheim,

had ... simplified the problem by replacing Lukàcs's position with a
genuine *pro domo plea*. Mannheim had replaced the pioneering consciousness of the revolutionary proletariat with a privileged group supposedly
endowed with adequate knowledge of reality. ... In concrete terms this
standpoint amounted to making truth the privilege of a certain number of
college graduates and sociologists.[1]

Raymond Aron himself shared this unsophisticated point of view and says: in speaking of the Intelligentsia, Mannheim "appeared to be thinking of intellectuals and professors in particular."[2] According to G. Gurvitch, Mannheim claimed that those intellectuals were exempt from any social conditioning of thought.[3] Vilfredo Pareto had been called, with some irony, "the Karl Marx of the bourgeoisie." For the above quoted critics Mannheim appears as the Karl Marx of academic "Mandarinate." That is not a very prestigious title; the author of *Ideology and Utopia* deserves better.

These critics gloss over the term *freischwebend*, which Mannheim certainly chose for good reason. A professor is a civil servant more or less well paid as the case may be; he is not as such a "rootless" person. The academics of Weimar Germany — Mannheim's supposed theoretical model — were a "deeply rooted," often conservative social stratum. In a pioneering article devoted to "the problem of generations," Mannheim spoke of "rootless men of letters" (*freischwebende Litteratenschicht*);[4] in his last work, *Freedom, Power and Democratic Planning*, he appealed to the "independent Intelligentsia," involved in careers outside the university, to combat the dangers of monotony and mediocrity typical of planned societies.[5] The proof seems conclusive: Mannheim was not thinking of his academic colleagues at all when he formulated this theory. The accent is on *freischwebend* rather than on *Intelligenz*.

This problem has an axiological aspect that may be overlooked in an overweighted cognitive interpretation. Ideology sits astride the ontological and axiological spheres (the *Sein* and the *Sollen*), and this lack of a clear distinction is an important factor of ideological distortion and occultation. In the Stalinist era, the ideological overestimation of Soviet social reality effectively blinded people to the existence of the Gulag, despite the concordant testimonies, which, as we now know, were fully reliable. According to the Hungarian philosopher Tibor Hanàk, a valid ideological critique "does not aim to negate the existence of value systems but merely underlines their non belonging to the sphere of rationality."[6] Praising members of one's ingroup is after all a normal attitude; it becomes an ideological one when this subjective overestimation is projected into the rationality of biological science and thereby appropriates the right to despise the "outgroup." Understandably, rootless intellectuals who live somewhat outside the mainstream, are in a good position to disentangle the axio-cognitive blurring of ideological discourse. It also is understandable that from a biased point of view they may appear to be destroyers of traditional values and "poisoners of public opinion." Here we are faced with one of the main reasons for the tenacious persistence of antisemitic prejudice in our contemporary societies. Gurvitch's above quoted interpretation is in my view symptomatic of a double misunderstanding. "Elite intellectuelle" is a mistranslation of *freischwebende Intelligenz,* and Mannheim was too knowledgeable a sociologist—and too close to Marxism—to seriously consider that belonging to a given social stratum could allow anybody to "think outside of social frameworks." In this perspective it is too easy for his detractors to say, with a touch of irony, that "like any other professional group, such as lawyers, priests shoemakers, etc" intellectuals "have individual, particular and general economic interests."[7] Mannheim and his critics do not speak the same language. Vested interest is not the only factor—not even the main one—of the process of ideologization. Mannheim is judged from the perspective of vulgar Marxism, whereas his principal merit is his constant striving to keep a distance from it.

Two other fundamental misunderstandings blur the issue. The "cognitive" interpretation of political alienation, advocated among others by Goldmann, reduces the phenomenon of false consciousness to a simple inaccuracy, i.e. to a socially determined tenacious error (*Ignorantia invincibilis*). Seen from this standpoint, academic scholarship may indeed function as a specific remedy; but false consciousness is a sui generis phenomenon akin to paranoid delusions; it really does not have much to do with the degree of information possessed by an individual or community.[8] Another source of misunderstanding is the supposed uniformity of the mechanisms of social determination of consciousness. In ordinary Marxism superstructures are dependent on infrastructures in a uniform manner, and "class interest" is supposed to be the main if not the sole motive of this dependence. Mannheim's concept of "socially determined thought" (*Seinsgebundenes Denken*) presupposes, on the contrary, a polyvalent set of varied mechanisms. This concept may include disparate factors such as the influence of techniques on science (with no distortion of the scientist's outlook) and the multiple forms of social egocentricity that often orient the logical structure of thought towards reification and "de-dialectization." It is not contradictory to assert that an intellectual's thinking may depend on the first mechanism while partly escaping the effects of the second. Now the fact is that the process of ideologization is located in the latter.

The distinction proposed by Anglo-Saxon authors, such as Werner Stark, between the social *origin* and social *determination* of knowledge may be called on to clarify the issue.[9] These terms have different connotations: "determination" implies a more active influence, in short a more alienating one. Saying that a point of view is social in origin is a simple statement; claiming that it is *determined by the social situation* implies a touch of criticism and even of suspicion. The postulate of the social origin of knowledge contains no elements of a possible distortion; it may be applied to exact sciences. The postulate of social determinaion of a point of view implies distortion or at least a fragmentary or biased vision. The notion of social origin refers to a supposedly homogenous society; social determination implies belonging to a class or to a fighting group. The unmasking of social origins is the main task of the sociology of knowledge; that of social determination focuses on the critique of ideology. Of the two schools that claim to be at the origin of the sociology of knowledge, Durkheimianism stresses the social origin of knowledge, whereas Marxism underlines the *determination* of ideologies by class situations. These two perspectives are complementary. Vulgar Marxism, which refuses to acknowledge the difference between the critique of ideology and the sociology of knowledge, tends to use "superstructure" and "ideology" as synonyms. This terminology needs to be refined: the notion of "superstructure" corresponds, in my view, to the social origin of thought, and "ideology" to its social *determination.*

Mannheim never claimed that intellectuals were capable of eliminating the social component of the cognitive process, but something else altogether; the thinking of rootless intellectuals, though it is "socially determined" (*Seinsverbunden*) contains decentralizing factors that make it more resistent to sociocentric distortion. Their thought is of social *origin*, but its social *determination* (and the concomitant risks of distortion and bias) is supposed to be less than for other strata. There is nothing contradictory in all this. For example, intellectuals are often polyglots for professional reasons: that is the *social origin.* Be that as it may, the command of several languages is a decentralizing factor that attenuates the *social determination* of thought: it is easier for polyglots to avoid succumbing to ready-made ideas than for those who speak only one language. Thus Mannheim does not suggest that we consider members of the Intelligentsia as supernatural beings with no personal needs or interests. He merely states that their sui generis sociability involves elements that facilitate the dialectical (totalizing) synthesis of various perspectives.

I take the liberty of giving a simplistic example. In a matter that has given rise to so many misunderstandings, no good example should be discarded no matter how elementary it may be. The statement, "The Tower of Pisa leans to the left" is neither true nor false; it is meaningless. On the other hand, the statement, "viewed from a certain spot, the tower appears to lean to the left" is a perfectly meaningful proposition, the validity of which is based on an exact definition of the relationship between the observer (the subject) and the observed phenomenon (the object). In Mannheim's terms, it is a "functionalized" statement. Mannheim considered that political knowledge is valid if, and only if, it is placed in perspective (i.e. "functionalized") in accordance with the observer's historical standpoint *(Standort)*. Once this functionalization has been carried out, it should be possible to change from one ideology to the other through an operation similar to translation,[10] through a process of synthesis followed by the extraction of a scientifically valid residue.[11] Such tasks are especially well-suited to the Intelligentsia, which is characterized not by teaching at a university or collecting parchments but by the ability to walk all the way around the Tower of Pisa. The "idealtype" of the rootless person is in my view the immigrant, the convert, and perhaps still more, the *naturalized citizen* i.e., persons who belong simultaneously to two different value systems whose alientating effects are so mutually counterbalanced. An impressive number of theorists of alienation and sociologists of knowledge are naturalized citizens and immigrants: Goldmann, Gurvitch, Mannheim, Pareto, Sorokine, Szende, and Znaniecki, to name but a few. Such intellectuals are sometimes professors with encyclopedic knowledge, but not always: Koestler, the epitome of this category, was never a professor, nor was Marx. They are sometimes bohemians who spend their lives in cafés, but that is not a general rule either. Some of the above-mentioned theorists held important positions, worked hard, and even led the high life. The essential criterion is "inner marginality," i.e. the ability to shift from one perspective to another. H. Speier saw this question clearly:

Mannheim does not claim that such intellectuals have direct access to truth. They are not immune to the social determination of thought; it is simply more complex in their case. Members of the "unattached Intelligentsia" are not "free" in the broad sense of the term; they are free to choose among various perspectives and to synthesize them.[12]

Aristotle the "metic" was probably the first great rootless intellectual in the history of ideas. Without slighting his genius, one might wonder whether the extraordinary "social awareness" of the author of *Politics*, is not a lucky result of this situation. Emperor Frederick II (1196–1250) is a similar case who demonstrates that it is possible to be a rootless intellectual on the throne. An exceptional polyglot for his time, the emperor mastered a number of languages and cultures, including Arabic. A genuine scholar, he "de-alienated" science by removing it from the sterilizing influence of scholasticism. His treatise *De arte venandi cum avibus* is three centuries before the *Novum Organum*, a paragon of empiric research. This monarch was of German origin, Italian by birth and by nature, allied with the Byzantine schismatics, and so taken by the Arabian culture and lifestyle that he asked to be buried in Oriental garb. His rootlessness explains his exceptional intellectual and political lucidity — as well as the ultimate failure of his projects.

His reign included a tragic episode. The imprisonment and the suicide of the imperial Lord Chancellor Pier della Vigna was a one of the most sensational events of the Middle Ages. Pier was the emperor's closest assistant and perhaps his only friend; his alleged treason has never been proved. During his voyage through Hell, Dante met Pier sentenced not as a traitor but as a suicide. He was turned into a tree. During their conversation he swore *by his new roots*[13] that he had never betrayed his master "who was so worthy of honor."

Now the status of the rootless may ultimately become uncomfortable. The rootless emperor's chancellor swearing by "his new roots" reminds one of Arthur Koestler, who wrote in one of his last books that he wanted henceforth to be considered as a "Briton." But one has to be accepted first.

The problem of the Intelligentsia, as it appears in Mannheim's work, is tied up with that of false consciousness and with the sociology of knowledge of dialectical thought. In a frequently quoted passage in the foreword of *The Capital*,[14] Marx claims that the conservative interest of the upper classes stands in the way of a dialectical ("historicist") understanding of social reality since the latter involves the awareness of the historical, i.e. precarious nature of their privileges. Now, according to young Marx's formulation, ideology (i.e. false consciousness) is primarily tantamount to a negation or distortion of history. As for the exploited classes, the "heirs to the future," historical time is their ally, they are thus supposed to be immune to false consciousness. Max Scheler, taking up this classical theme of mainstream Marxism, claimed that the political consciousness of the upper classes leans towards "considerations of being" (*Seinsbetrachtung*), whereas the lower classes are more concerned with "considerations of becoming" (*Werdensbetrachtung*).[15] It is noteworthy that in Marx's *The Capital*, dialectic appears exlusively as *Werdensbetrachtung*, i.e. as virtually synonymous with historicism.[16] The gnoseo-sociological incidences of the dialectic of concrete totality (Lukàcs) are not in the foreground of Marx's thought, at least not in this often-quoted passage.

Things have changed since the publication of Marx's famous preface. The ideological episode of Stalinism proved that the proletariat's alleged immunity to false consciousness is a myth: the actual political consciousness of the working class is also subject to de-dialectizing influences through mechanisms other than the self-interested blind spot to historical time peculiar to the upper classes, according to Marx and Scheler. When socialist ideals take the form of state power, the working class's consciousness of its historical mission can turn into collective egocentricity (sociocentricity). Now egocentricity on both the individual and collective scales is instrumental in reification and de-dialectization of mental processes. It appears that both aspects of the dialectic — the "dialectics of becoming" and the "dialectics of totality" — are in different gnoseo-sociological situations, and this paradoxical fact is probably one reason for the "Adventures of the Dialectics" (title of a well-known work by the French philosopher M. Merleau-Ponty). Conservative self-interest can indeed act as an ideological barrier against the awareness of the necessity of social change; we saw it, not very long ago, in the debate on decolonization. On the other hand, collective egocentricity can lead to a "schizoid approach," i.e. a fragmented, dissociated, non-totalizing grasp of political reality. It may be argued that the proletariat as the "lower" class is particularly open to the *Werdensbetrachtung*. As for the perception of concrete historical totalities (*Ganzheitsbetrachtung*) the proletarian *Stan-*

*dort* (i.e. the position of the working class in the historical process) may appear as a handicap. All the advantages in the field of dialectics that the working class is supposed to obtain from its socially determined (*seinsverbunden*) acceptation of social change may be counterbalanced by the emergence of a sociocentric logic, involving a "privileged system," and such a logic is diametrically opposed to dialectics. Stalinist ideology was the extreme form of this phenomenon. Mannheim's theory of the rootless Intelligentsia is worthy of more than mere irony; it is the legitimate cry of alarm of a free spirit confronted with the rise of totalitarian mentality which seemed unstoppable at the time

The aim of this chapter is to contrast an adequate description of this often criticized aspect of Mannheim's theory with the caricatural picture given by his detractors, such as the late Lucien Goldmann. I do not mean that the Mannheim thesis is beyond criticism. It is easy to call to mind the blind spot of distinguished intellectuals and "fellow travellers" to the "Stalinist phenomenon" or, closer to us, the lack of perspicacity of outstanding members of the Parisian Intelligentsia, like Michel Foucault, with respect to recent events in Iran. Intellectuals often have a tendency to fight off the anxiety of isolation by over identifying with foreign causes, adopting their (sometimes inadequate) historical perspective and introjecting the corollary forms of false consciousness. Mannheim indicated this phenomenon without grasping its full importance.[17] We are here faced with one of the limits of the validity of his theory. Nonetheless this theory contains valuable elements of an anticipated critique of extreme forms of political alienation (such as Stalinism among others), destined to play an important role in postwar France's intellectual life. Mannheim foreshadows Orwell but in this question his political lucidity was more precocious than that of the renowned author of "1984."

# Notes

1. L. Goldmann, *Sciences humaines et philosophie* (Paris: P.U.F., 1952), 38 (italics ours).
2. R. Aron, *La Sociologie allemande contemporaine* (Paris: P.U.F., 1950), 88 (italics ours).
3. G. Gurvitch, "Le problème de la sociologie de la connaissance," *Revue Philosophique*, octobre-décembre 1958, 326.

4. K. Mannheim, "Das Problem der Generationen," *Kölner Vierteljahrshefte für Soziolgie*, 1928, 326.
5. "A democratic society should deliberately plan for careers outside the regular social and educational ladders" (Mannheim, *Freedom, Power and Democratic Planning* [New York: Oxford University Press, 1950], 264–65).
6. Tibor Hanàk, *Ideologies and our Time* (in Hungarian) (London: Szepsi Csombor kör, 1969), 18.
7. L. Goldmann, *Sciences humaines*, 39.
8. The false consciousness of "fellow travellers" is a good example of this aspect of ideologization. See David Caute, *Les compagnons de Route*.
9. Werner Stark stressed the importance of this distinction and emphasized the necessity of drawing the boundary between the sociology of knowledge and the "Ideologiekritik." See W. Stark, *The Sociology of Knowledge* (Glencoe: The Free Press, 1958), 172.
10. The idea of a "translation" from one ideological system to another is formulated by Mannheim in his article "Wissenssoziologie" (1931). This article was reprinted as an appendix to the English and German editions (1965) of *Ideology and Utopia*.

    Raymond Aron considered this attempt to be absurd. "One cannot change from one interpretation of the world to another. The Marxist interpretation and the liberal interpretation of an economic fact cannot be reconciled. There are no points of equivalence to be established because they are two contradictory interpretations that cannot therefore be accepted simultaneously" (Aron, *La Sociologie allemande*, 88–9).

    This judgment is a bit hasty. F. Hayek writes that "nobody understood better than Tocqueville that democracy, being an essentially individualist institution, was unreconciliable with socialism" (Hayek, *La route de la servitude* [Paris: Librairie de Médicis, 1945], 70). Here is a "translation" into Marxist language: "Nobody understood better than Lenin that socialism being an essentially collective institution could not be reconciled with democracy." That is exactly the same statement viewed in a different axiological context (in a different *Wertbeziehung* in Max Weber's terminology); it remains ideological. Their common denominator is that the edification of socialism is incompatible with pluralist democracy; that is no longer an ideological statement, but an objective observation borne out by history and by experience of everyday life.
11. In his late works Mannheim advocated the idea of "democratic planning" (planning for freedom). The underlying idea of this suggestion was that planning-oriented policy, which is part of the ideologies of both left- and right-wing extremes, must be valid independent of the conflicting ideologies.

12. Speier, review of "Ideology and Utopia," *American Journal of Sociology* (July 1937).
13. "Per le nove radici d'esto legno / vi giuro, che giá mai no ruppi fede / al mio signor, che fu d'onor si degno" (Dante, *Inferno*, Canto XIII).
14. "The mystic aspect of dialectics became fashionable in Germany because it seemed to glorify the existing state of things. Its rational aspect was seen as a scandal and an abomination by the ruling classes and their doctrinaire ideologues because in the primitive conception of things it includes the awareness of their final disappearance. . . . Nothing would be able to impose it since it is essentially critical and revolutionary." (*The Capital*, foreword).
15. Max Scheler, *Die Wissensformen und die Gesellschaft* (Leipzig: Neuer Geist Verlag, 1926), 204 ff.
16. See this curious definition of dialectics by Lukàcs: "Wissenschaft der Geschichte in ihrem einmaligen unwiderholbaren Ablauf" (the science of history considered in its unique, unrepeatable course). Quoted by Ernst Grünwald, *Das Problem der Soziologie des Wissens* (Wien-Leipzig, Braumüller Verlag, 1934), 128.
17. Mannheim *Ideologie und Utopie*, (1965), 124.

# 7

# Mannheim's Second Period
# (Writings in Emigration)

Mannheim's English works are disappointing in comparison to his writings of the Weimar period.[1] They have had little impact in France where they are rarely quoted even in general surveys, such as the one by Jacques J. Maquet or by Georg Gurvitch.[2] Compared to his preceding period, these works reveal more practical preoccupations, such as the problem of democratic planning. Mannheim remained, however, a Marxist during this period of his career; except for a few concessions in terminology, he carried over the essential of the dialectical themes of his German writings. It seems that his ambition, somewhat paradoxical, was to put positive accomplishments of Marxism (in particular the dialectical critique of ideologies) to the service of liberal democracy, diagnosed by him, with good reason at this time, as suffering from a dangerous vulnerability in the ideological competition with the socialist camp.

In the academic circles of the Weimar Republic, Mannheim has been considered, with some perspicacity, as a "bourgeois Marxist" at a time when in fact he had not yet become one. In his emigration period he actually became a bourgeois Marxist, the "Marxist" of a bourgeoisie who, under historical constraint, made — particularly in the United States — some substantial concessions to the spirit of socialism. The historical significance of these concessions was to become one of the main themes of the American political debate during the fifties, some years after Mannheim's death. Mannheim's English works involve an anticipated dialectical and historicist critique of

McCarthyism and Goldwaterism which are, as I argue elsewhere, specific American aspects of the phenomenon of false consciousness.[3]

The comparison with Lukàcs is significant and illustrates an important aspect of the ideological situation in the postwar period. Lukàcs was forced to give up his role as critical theorist of ideology in order to be able to accept, as a militant, the progressive ideologization of official Marxism. His recantation of *History and Class Consciousness* has probably no other reason. Stalinism was a genuine "ideal-type" of false consciousness; after Orwell, Aron, and many others, this has now become evident, but it was not so in the early fifties. "On ne parle pas de corde dans la maison d'un pendu" as the French saying goes. Mannheim's fate was just the opposite to that of Lukàcs. In his Anglo-Saxon period he experienced no difficulty in remaining a dialectical theorist of ideology as he had been in pre-Hitlerite Germany. He only had to disguise his vocabulary so as not to shock a new public allergic to Marxism. His concessions were of secondary importance, whereas those of Lukàcs were essential. It appears that the superstructures of postwar capitalism were less ideologized than those of the Socialist camp under Stalin and Jdanov.

After the Second World War capitalism — American capitalism in particular — underwent a sufficiently profound transformation to justify the emergence of a new concept: "neo-capitalism." That change was due to several converging causes: labor pressure, continuation of the special measures required by the war effort, and — last but not least — the ideological challenge of the Socialist camp, which had become particularly dangerous in the light of the immense prestige enjoyed at this time by the Soviet Union, considered as the principal architect of the common victory. This necessary and, all in all, beneficial transformation (the emergence of neo-capitalism) nonetheless created serious problems of "awareness" in American ultraconservative circles, which were chiefly represented at this time by the right wing of the G.O.P. Such conservatives considered American neo-capitalism to be a "slow-working form" of communism resulting from the action of obscure anti-American forces. McCarthyism — and later Goldwaterism — are convincing illustrations of the anti-historicism of ideological discourse. Barry Goldwater blamed the American educational system for having turned schools into "laboratories of socio-economic change."[4] His criticism of the foreign policy of the Democratic administration in Washington was based on criteria that were perfectly valid at the time of McKinley, president of a United States invulnerable to military attack, but were out of date in the epoch of intercontinental rockets. Similarly, McCarthy in 1952 blamed the U.S. forces of occupation in Japan for having released in 1945 the survivors of the Sorge spy-ring,[5] who had been working for a country allied to the United States at the time. Such anti-historicism involves a *magical* conception of political responsibility, based on the tacit assumption of an omnipotent government acting in a socio-historical vacuum and an anti-historical perception of individual existence reminiscent of the underlying ideology of the Moscow Trials.[6] Just as in Prosecutor Vichinsky's eyes today's traitor has always been a traitor, the McCarthyist president of the Senatorial Commission on Unamerican Activities thought that once a Communist, always a Communist. McCarthyism was a sort of mirror image of Stalinism, for which it probably had an unconscious fascination. It was also self-destructive: the chronic unpopularity of American policy in Western intellectual circles is largely the aftermath of McCarthyism in the fifties; the reader need only read Bertrand Russell's admirable essay in *Nightmares.*[7]

Mannheim's work is an anticipated criticism to these distortions of the "American Ideology." He strived to become a political psychoanalyst of American democracy, which suffered from anti-dialectical and anti-historicist neurosis. He tempted to smuggle some dialectic (more Marxist than Hegelian) into the ideological framework of liberalism. In 1927 Karl August Wittfogel — future author of a world-famous polemic against communism but a staunch Marxist at this time — decried the "sociologists of knowledge who [like Mannheim] pillage the scientific arsenal of the class enemy."[8] In conservative public opinion, such ideological turncoats might have been taken for poisoners. Thus, Mannheim was careful to present his dialectical medicine in flasks with innocent-looking labels. In his English works, the dialectic is never mentioned by name; moreover, an attempt was made to place it within the reach of minds with little training in philosophical reflection. From the standpoint of contemporary French academia, some of his suggestions might appear banal, but his effort has the right to be judged in its own context.

The problem of *education for change* is one of the major leitmotifs in his English writings. In the past, schools had often been a conservative force; according to Mannheim they have to become a *factor of change* in the new democracy. "Democratic personality welcomes disagreement because it has the courage to expose itself to change."[9] Mannheim seems to challenge in advance the opinion of Barry Goldwater that I quoted. His suggestions were elementary, it is true, but they responded *in this elementary form* to a specific urgent need for political de-alienation demonstrated a few years later by the emergence of McCarthyist political delusion, which was so particularly harmful to the image of American democracy throughout the world.

The concept of the *dialectical totality,* which plays an essential role in the thinking of Lukàcs, is naturally missing from Mannheim's English terminology; it is replaced by "wholeness" or "synthetic view" which means exactly the same thing. This concept along with the theme of "education for change" are the two major leitmotifs of his English works. The "bourgeois Marxist" sets himself a difficult task — to make pluralistic democracy aware of its dialectical needs and possibilities despite a public strongly conditioned against Marxism. His writings therefore offer a vulgarized form of Marxism, but they have nothing in common with vulgar Marxism, which is essentially characterized by an emphasis on the materialist side of Marxism over the dialectical one. Not only did Mannheim not abandon the dialectic in his English works, he even became a more consistent dialectician than in his Weimar writings. The term "false consciousness" rarely appears; as we have seen, it was frequently disguised — perhaps with the author's consent — in the English translation of *Ideology and Utopia.* The *concept* of false consciousness is nonetheless present, albeit under a pseudonym. The term *split consciousness,* which appears frequently, is a clear allusion to it; the same holds true for the expression "society blindness," commonly used in the texts of that period. Von Wiese called Mannheim the "most determined sociologist among German writers";[10] for Mannheim, the simple fact of refusing a sociological understanding of data (what is now called "methodological individualism") reveals the first steps towards an ideological attitude. "The basic impact of his views," writes Paul Kecskeméti, "is not some new discovery in the social sciences but the fact that he stresses the importance and meaning of sociology as an *intellectual attitude.* Sociology has always included a particular 'pathic' dimension; not satisfied with having attained the status of a science, sociology claims to be the radical remedy for the 'poverty of philosophy.' "[11] Those lines, penned in 1926, are particularly applicable to Mannheim's attitude during his Anglo-Saxon period. As far as sociologism is tantamount to "de-alienation," then it follows that society blindness is by definition an alienating attitude that fosters false consciousness. Nevertheless, this concept of "society blindness" is a little vague since it covers such disparate phenomena as liberal consciousness and racist consciousness.[12] The use of this term in the works of his Anglo-Saxon period did not show any progress over the major themes of his German works, but at least it attests to their permanence.

An interesting chapter of his *Diagnosis of our time* devoted to the problem of *social awareness* is a coherent exposition of the problem of false consciousness naturally without employing the "taboo" Marxist terminology.[13] Social awareness is the opposite of society blindness. By "awareness" Mannheim does not mean,

the mere accumulation of rational knowledge. Awareness means both in the life of the individual and in that of the community the readiness to see the whole situation in which one finds oneself, and not only to orientate one's action on immediate tasks and purposes but to base them on a more comprehensive vision. One of the ways in which awareness expresses itself is *the correct diagnosis of a situation* .[14]

I should like to point out that one of the French vanguard movements in 1968, characterized by its clearly de-alienating tendency, called itself "mouvement situationniste."

This leads us to the inevitable psychoanalytic example: an intelligent young man, perfectly capable of facing immediate problems may, at the same time, be *unaware* of certain latent anxieties that are paralyzing him. By finding out the psychological category to which he belongs or the true sources of his anxieties, he may be able to cope with the situation.[15] An old peasant who has never left his village is capable of orienting himself in his limited universe; however, he lacks *awareness*, since he takes the social roles of his "limited universe" to be absolute laws of life in general. He would have difficulty adapting to city life, but if he succeeded, he would have the opportunity of attaining a *higher* awareness involving the possibility of two coexistent, parallel worlds: the country and the city.[16]

Another example—which is not one of Mannheim's—of attaining higher awareness is learning a foreign language for the first time. Such learning is a type of de-alienation since it involves a de-reification of the structures of one's mother tongue, which tend to be mistaken for real, objective features of reality. Thus the polyglottism of intellectuals — especially of "rootless" ones such as immigrants and naturalized citizens — contributes to de-reification, which is reminiscent of one of the major themes of *Ideology and Utopia.*

Obviously, *lack of social awareness* is the "bourgeois version" of false consciousness. An old peasant who considers the social structure of his village to be a universal one, harbors the same sort of illusion as a worker "with no class consciousness" who perceives the reified economic laws of the capitalist system as natural laws. This concept is also related to Goldmann's notion of *conscience possible.* In fact, awareness "does not claim the knowledge of transcendental things which are beyond human experience, such as ghosts, spirits, or even the divinity, but of facts which are ready to become part of experience yet which do not enter into the picture because somehow we do not want to take congizance of them."[17]

Class consciousness is a form of partial awareness[18] involving two elements: a realistic awareness of the factors helping one group to fight against another and a covering-up of factors likely to lead to reconciliation. In other words, it is the partial vision of the social universe characteristic of a fighting group. The proletarian consciousness perceives socialist solutions, but it tends to have a blind spot for nonsocialist ones. The undeniable economic and social attainments of American neo-capitalism in the immediate postwar period shocked the consciousness of European workers. This fact explains, at least in part, the paradoxical anti-Americanism of European workers. Mannheim called out for greater awareness through the integration of partial experiences; in this respect, he stayed very close to the program drawn up in 1929 in *Ideologie und Utopie.*

The degree of awareness required by a given society varies according to its historical circumstances. Mannheim never made a secret of his admiration for the Anglo-Saxon lifestyle. But this attractive lifestyle, with its penchant for safety and gradual social changes and its tendency to avoid thorny debates and shocking subjects, threatens to make its adherents ideologically defenseless against the proponents of abrupt social changes and brutal statements of the facts: the totalitarians. "Today we realize that during the last decades a collective delusion prevailed in Western Democracies which consisted in an attitude of first ignoring and then denying the existence of menacing facts such as the rise and the growth of the Fascist regimes in Italy and Germany."[19] According to Mannheim, the "appeasement policy" of Neville Chamberlain, as well as the propaganda for unilateral disarmament in certain left-wing circles, was symptomatic of this *lack of awareness*, i.e. of false consciousness.[20] Such issues are still relevant in 1990.

World War II created a new situation. Economic planning, previously considered to be a collectivist or totalitarian technique, became a necessity for wartime democracies. It would have been naive to believe that once victory had been assured, democracies would go back to the laissez-faire system (Mannheim was particularly prophetic when he who wrote these lines in 1943). A third road came into view: economic planning without dictatorship, combined with a striving for social justice without abstract egalitarianism. When democracies emerged from this test, they had become more socialist, and the dominant struggle in capitalism was no longer "capitalism versus socialism" but "democratic planning versus totalitarian planning." The actors in that drama followed outmoded ideologies. Mannheim said that

> The main theme of history became different and it is only due to a lack of awareness that all the parties still repeat their catch-phrases and do not dare to identify themselves entirely with the cause for which they make limitless sacrifice and for which they are already fighting.[21] In this struggle we shall either be able to produce the necessary awareness which turns the tragedy of war into a creative venture in social reconstruction — or we shall perish.[22]

Thus, Mannheim foresaw the possibility of a general process of economic de-reification and ideological de-alienation in the context of neo-capitalism, which he felt coming, although he never used that term. Such views, which were typical of his "bourgeois Marxist" attitude, naturally shocked orthodox Marxists. According to Lukàcs, economic de-reification is exclusively within the historical domain of the proletariat. In his view, simply admitting its possibility in a capitalist context showed a form of false consciousness: "The supreme degree of unconsciousness, the most blatant form of 'false consciousness' [of the bourgeoisie] is always expressed through the growing illusion that economic phenomena are consciously controlled."[23] History has doubly refuted the author of *History and Class Conscious-*

*ness* while at least partially confirming Mannheim's predictions. First of all, "proletarian" planning has not eliminated the danger of false consciousness, as proved by Stalinism. Secondly, the hypothesis of a "conscious mastery" of economic effects outside a proletarian context (in other words, the idea of democratic planning advocated by Mannheim) has turned out to be less illusory than it may have appeared to Marxists in 1923 or even 1939.

Mannheim's English-language works did not get a very warm welcome in France. The disordered structure of these writings, the repetitions and the sometimes excessive simplicity of his often dull discourse make for difficult reading. It must be said that these works probably belong to his period of decline; he died only a few years later, at the age of fifty-four. Moreover, they were written during his second emigration; even for the theorist of the rootless Intelligentsia, two changes of homeland during a short existence are perhaps too many. His last work in English, his "sociological testament," *Freedom, Power and Democratic Planning*, was put into final form posthumously by his friends; the book shows the inevitable signs of that reverent task.

However, those works are better than they are reputed to be. Mannheim, purely a theorist in Germany, obviously tried *to make himself useful* in the Anglo-Saxon world. He intended to transplant the critique of ideology that flourished in Weimar Germany to Anglo-Saxon soil in order to contribute to the defense of democracy. It was an ambitious project that probably exceeded his possibilities: *in magnis et voluisse sat est*. Of course, the excessive simplicity of his discourse is still annoying, but, without pointing out once again the English readership's lack of receptiveness to abstract discourses, it is important to remember that false consciousness itself is often on a primitive level, as well. It sometimes assumes the deceptive form of anti-dialectical "common sense," governed by the principle of identification; part of its attractiveness is due to the intellectual comfort it offers to lazy minds. The falsity of consciousness is often based on a refusal to carry out simple socio-dialectical functional analysis. In his German writings, Mannheim showed himself amply capable of subtlety and abstract thought. The purpose of his English writings seems to be to fight false consciousness on its own level. Mannheim may have been thinking of the tragic example of the Weimar Republic in which the masses sank into the most barbarous form of political alienation despite the brilliant insights into alienation to be found within its intellectual ivory towers.

It should also be noted that Mannheim's German writings took form at a time of political crisis, whereas his English writings probably reflect a psychological and moral crisis of a *personal nature*. He was probably severely affected by the fall of Weimar democracy. That ephemeral democratic experiment was a curious chapter of modern history, resulting in a blossoming nonconformist culture *(Kulturbolschevismus)*, highly inclined to theorizing about problems but defenseless when it came to coping with practical ones. Mannheim's German writings show how much he, a naturalized German citizen himself, had made that agitated world his intellectual homeland; he sometimes gives the impression of being naively proud to belong to it. The brutal crumbling of that world must have affected Mannheim at a much deeper level than its immediate meaning for his personal existence.

The rise of national socialism probably had another traumatic aspect for Mannheim. Besides the shock that he received as a Jewish academic abruptly forced to emigrate, the scientific interpretation of the fascist phenomenon—which reached its peak under Hitler—posed new problems for the sociologist and philosopher. All of Mannheim's efforts had been directed at achieving a higher synthesis of half-truths each of which was fully true when considered from a certain historical standpoint *(Standort)*. The rise of national socialism confirmed the failings of his viewpoint; racism is not an ideology like the others, but an insane theory of a criminal practice. National socialism, a Manichean structure, itself, imposed a certain degree of Manicheism on its opponents, thereby indirectly contributing to the rebirth of various forms of false consciousness in the postwar period.[24] Moreover, according to the strong formulation of Mannheim's views by Paul Kecskeméti, "saying no to History, even in the darkest moment, would have meant saying no to Man and even to God."[25] Historicism as a philosophical credo is of course incompatible with totalitarian mentality (refer to *1984* by George Orwell), but historicists are bound, by their very doctrine, to understand totalitarianism in historicist terms, as difficult as that may be. In this perspective, totalitarianism appears to be a false, often atrocious, answer to *real* problems. Mannheim tried to deduce some helpful findings from it for his great idea of "democratic planning." This aspect of his work required an exceptional degree of intellectual courage.[26]

He had also to undergo the shock of his first contact with the Anglo-Saxon democracies. Unlike Weimar, Anglo-Saxon political life was not inclined to self-analysis or to reflection on sophisticated ideological problems but these democracies ran smoothly thanks to the public spiritedness of their peoples. What was probably lacking in Weimar was the straightforward respect that the average U.S. citizen professes for his constitution and the Englishman for his monarch, which amounts to the same thing. There was no need for exceptional "awareness" to foresee the rôle to be played by Anglo-Saxon democracies in the struggle against totalitarianism. It might have taken more foresight to predict the seriousness of their ideological handicaps, which did not come to light until the postwar period. Mannheim, a sworn enemy of conformism, must have been dreaming of a great synthesis—a democracy as efficient as the United States' and as non-conformist as Weimar at its beginning in the twenties. That was an attractive, but chimerical, combination; the nonconformist mentality that takes root in unsolved problems, is frequently symptomatic of the failure of democracy. But to the American mind, which was predominantly conformist at the time, Mannheim offered, if not an example, at least a warning.

## Notes

1. The works in question are *Diagnosis of Our Time* (New York: Oxford University Press, 1944), and *Freedom, Power and Democratic Planning* by the same publisher, 1950. *Mensch und Gesellschaft im Zeitalter des Umbaus* appeared in German while he was already in exile (Leiden, 1935); the English translation (*Man and Society in an Age of Reconstrution* [New York: Harcourt Brace, 1940; and in: Routledge & Kegan Paul, 1954]) included several hitherto unpublished chapters. That work was therefore the transition between the two major stages in Mannheim's career.

2. Jacques J. Maquet, *La Sociologie de la Connaissance* (Louvain: E. Nauwelaerts, 1940), et G. Gurvitch, "Le problème de la sociologie de la connaissance," *Revue Philosophique* 82, 4 (1957): 494–502.

3. For greater detail, the reader may refer to my two papers "The Meaning of McCarthyism" and "The False Consciousness of a Conservative" pub-

lished in *La Revue Socialiste* in 1954 and 1964, respectively, and re-published in *Idéologies* (Paris: Anthropos, 1974), 205–43.

4. Barry Goldwater, *The Conscience of a Conservative* (New York: Mac-fadden-Bartell, 1963), 86.

5. Joseph McCarthy, *The fight for America* (New York: Devin-Adair, 1952).

6. A "magical" conception of political responsibility postulates at the base of government action not at all a "praxis" in a dialectical relationship with the historical context, but a magical action independent of this context and supposed to enjoy omnipotence. One of the great themes of McCarthyism in the 1950s was the defeat of Nationalist China by the Communist forces of Mao-Tse-Tung, arbitrarily attributed to the "treason" of the Democrats in power at that time.

7. Bertrand Russell, *Nightmares of Eminent Persons and Other Stories* (London: Badley Head, 1954).

8. Karl August Wittfogel, "Wissen und Gesellschaft. Neuere deutsche Litteratur zur Wissenssoziologie," *Unter dem Banner des Marxismus*, 1931 Vol V, fasc. 1, 83–102.

9. K. Mannheim, *Freedom, Power and Democratic Planning* (New York: Oxford University Press, 1950), 201 ff.

10. L. Von Wiese, "Karl Mannheim," *Kölner Zeitschrift für Soziologie*, Vol 1, fasc. 1, 1948–49, "Er war unter deutschen Schriftstellern der entschiedenste Soziologist."

11. Paul Kecskeméti, "A szociologia történetfilozofiai megalapitàsa: Karl Mannheim," *(Szàzadunk* [Our Century], 1926, 456 [Budapest]: The philosophy of history as a foundation of sociology: Karl Mannheim).

12. Obviously, racist consciousness, as a form of false consciousness, partakes of both ahistoricism and asociologism (society-blindness). Mannheim defines liberal consciousness as a form of (false?) unconditioned consciousness *(Unbedingtheitsbewusstsein)*, which he opposes to the "historically determined consciousness" *(Bedingtheitsbewusstsein)* of conservatives *(Ideology and Utopia*, 199). These examples show the utility of the concept of society-blindness and at the same time the limits of its utility.

13. Mannheim, *Diagnosis of Our Time* (New York: Oxford University Press, 1944), pp. 59–79 (Education, sociology, and the problem of social awareness).

14. Ibid., 67.

15. Ibid. The allusion to the psychoanalytical cure is clear, although not formulated explicitly. Mannheim's wife was a psychoanalyst.

16. Ibid., 68.

17. Mannheim, *Diagnosis,* 67. This is indeed false consciousness, but con-

trary to the interpretation by the present author, it is perceived in a psychoanalytical optic rather than a psychiatric one.

18. Mannheim, *Diagnosis,* 69.

19. Ibid., 72.

20. The resistance of almost all classes in this country to certain types of awareness is due not only to the happy continuity of its history which made possible a gradual adjustment to changing conditions, but also a deliberate avoidance of every opportunity which might lead to a clear statement of the issues at stake. For this one cannot blame certain individuals or classes only. The conservatives were as responsible as those progressives who discussed pacifism when the enemy was at the gates. The appeasement policy of Chamberlain is just another feature of the same unwillingness to face unpleasant facts which prevailed in British Labour circles who refused to rearm when they could have foreseen the results of unpreparedness (Ibid., 70–1).

These lines were written in 1943! They might have been written only yesterday. Today's English Labour Party leaders would do well to read Mannheim.

21. Ibid., 75.

22. Ibid., 79 ff.

23. G. Lukàcs, *Histoire et Conscience de Classe* (Paris: Ed. de Minuit, 1961), 89. German edition, Berlin, 1923, 76.

24. The morally inevitable Manicheism in the Nazi era ("There are the Nazis and the others") laid the way for an opposite form of Manicheism that predominated in the immediate postwar period in Stalinist Communist parties and among the "fellow-travellers." In the work by David Caute, *Les Compagnons de Route* (Paris, Robert Laffont, 1979), one finds a curious statement highly symptomatic of this manichean distortion of political awareness: "To claim that those men (the defendants of the Moscow Trials) are innocent is to accept Hitler's thesis and all its implications. Those who doubt this or that . . . imply forthwith . . . that it was not Hitler who had the Reichstag burned down. They proclaim Hitler and the Gestapo innocent of the Spanish Rebellion, and deny the Fascist intervention in Spain." Generally speaking, one of the traits of false consciousness is to create mirror phenomena, perpetuating false consciousness in the enemy camp. McCarthyism was a mirror phenomenon of the Stalinism it claimed to be fighting.

25. P. Kecskeméti in his preface to Mannheim, *Essays on the Sociology of Knowledge* (London: Routledge and Kegan, 1952), 2.

26. This could well explain the curious nods of approval that Mannheim, the democrat, professed to certain totalitarian "successes," especially in the field of education. Cf. *Freedom, Power and Democratic Planning*, 184; and *Diagnosis of Our Time*, 52.

# 8

# Utopian Consciousness

Utopia is traditionally defined as an unattainable project. M. Raymond Ruyer's fine book *L'Utopie et les utopies* demonstrates that this definition, despite its conventionality, lends itself to lofty philosophical considerations.[1]

Mannheim's research is based on a different criterion: "transcendence of social being" (*Seinstranszendenz*). As we have seen above, the English term "situationally transcendent" is a mistranslation that distorts Mannheim's message.[2] The expression *utopisches Bewusstsein* (utopian consciousness) was translated as utopian mentality, which further blurs the relationships between utopian consciousness and false consciousness.

The issue was clearly stated in the German editions of *Ideology and Utopia*. "The concepts of ideology and utopia have one common and essential point, in the final analysis: they both postulate the possible existence of false consciousness."[3] This passage met with some strange misfortunes; it disappeared from the French and English translations and reappeared in the German edition in 1965. In an article published in 1969, I blamed the translators for that omission;[4] it is possible, however, that Mannheim expressly requested it. His initial plan in the Weimar period was probably to use the concepts of false consciousness and *Seinstranscendenz* to bridge a gap between ideology and utopia. When Mannheim became aware of their incompatibility — either spontaneously or through the influence of his Anglo-Saxon colleagues — he chose to abandon the first concept for the second. I shall try to show that he should have done the opposite: the category of false consciousness may serve as a common denominator of Mannheim's two central concepts, provided that the fruitless criterion of the "transcendance of social being" is rejected.

The problem of Zionist *utopia* is a good example of the difficulties in Mannheim's approach. In F*reiheit und Ordnung* published in 1946, Ernst Bloch,[5] whose viewpoints are close to Mannheim's, dedicated a chapter to Theodor Herzl's *Altneuland*; in Raymond Ruyer's book, which was published four years later, there is no mention of it. Obviously between 1946 and 1950 there was 1948. Before the creation of the Hebrew state, the Zionist project seemed to correspond to Mannheim's definition of utopia; no political project had ever been more "transcendent of social being" than the one intended to transform Eastern ghetto dwellers into free citizens of a modern democracy. Forty years later, there is no denying that the Zionist project was not at all utopian and that the underlying political consciousness had nothing in common with false consciousness. A political project can therefore be "transcendent of social being" without being utopian; Ruyer's book points out typcial utopias that are in no way transcendent of social being. The ephemeral state of the Khmers Rouges in Cambodia featured many utopian characteristics but could it possibly be called a "transcendent of social being"?[6]

Can the concept of false consciousness furnish the common denominator that Mannheim requested in vain, from the criterion "transcendence of social being." To answer this question, I am obliged to refer to my personal interpretation of the problem of ideology, as stated in a number of articles published between 1947 and 1983,[7] and in more detail in my book *False Consciousness*. In my interpretation, clinical schizophrenia—in particular, the variety that E. Minkowski called "rationalisme et géometrisme morbides"—is, as reified consciousness, an individual form of false consciousness, whereas false consciousness of groups is a type of collective schizophrenia.

Pierre Ansart summed up my theory with the precision and clarity that are his own:

J. Gabel's comparison between schizophrenia and certain ideologies such as fascism under Hitler and Stalinism illustrates a new possibility of describing extreme forms of political pathology. A number of schizophrenic symptoms can indeed be found in such rationalizations and reveal forms of collective insanity. As in schizophrenia, such ideologies proceed ac-

cording to a "logic of identification," defining being by itself, and project-
ing completely dereistic identities. Those ideologies rely on forms of reification, as shown, in particular, by the deluded manner in which they perceive their enemies, which, according to the logic of such ideologies, lose
all of their own characteristics and become evil essences. In this kind of
rationalization, the forms of control of dialectical reason give way to non-
dialectical hallucinations in thinking.[8]

This interpretation provides a common denominator to the concepts
of ideology and utopia as expressions of false consciousness: it thus
becomes possible to keep the promise made by Mannheim in *Ideology
and Utopia*. The world of the utopia, as commonly defined, i.e. the
"subrealistic" utopia in the suggested terminology, does indeed have a
schizophrenic structure. François Laplantine speaks expressly of "political schizophrenia."[9] "Utopians" are no rarety in insane asylums.[10]
Raymond Ruyer's thorough analysis of utopian consciousness brings
to light most of the clinical symptoms of that form of mental illness: a
rigid vision of the world, illusions of omnipotence, anti-dialectical
academicism, lack of human warmth, etc.[11] The concepts of ideology
and utopia are both "subrealistic" (reified) perceptions of the present
and past, and in the latter case of the future. Simone de Beauvoir
spoke significantly of an "avenir-chose" (reified future). This does not
mean that the "surrealistic" concept of utopia is utterly worthless but
it is closer to the social myth than to utopia. According to the interpretation of Lukàcs, false consciousness is a *corollary of alienation;* an
individual or collective desire to "transcend social being" may be
tantamount to de-alienation rather than alienation. One can love or
hate the State of Israel; no one could seriously claim that contemporary Israelis are more "alienated" than the Jews who formerly lived in
ghettos.

Mannheim distinguishes four stages in the development of utopian
consciousness: the chiliastic, humanitarian-liberal, conservative, and
socialist-communist stages. His analysis of liberal and socialist utopia
is of limited originality. The concept of the "conservative utopia"
poses some interesting theoretical problems, as does that of the "reactionary utopia," which was not considered by Mannheim but which
could be analysed in the same context.[12]

According to Mannheim "in the liberal utopia, in the humanitarian
idea as contrasted with Chiliastic ecstasy, there is a relative approxi-

mation to the 'here and now.' In conservatism, we find the process of approximation to the 'here and now' completed. The utopia in this case is, from the very beginning, embedded in existing reality.

To this, obviously, there corresponds the fact that reality, the "here and now," is no longer experienced as an "evil" reality but as the embodiment of the highest values and meanings."[13]

That does not fit in with the definition of utopia by Mannheim who limits the meaning of the term "to that type of orientation which transcends reality and which at the same time breaks the bonds of the existing order"[14] Mannheim admits that conservatives have no genuine utopia since they consider social reality to be nonproblematic, in conformity with natural law.[15] The creation of a conservative counter-utopia (Gegenutopie) is nothing but a defensive reaction to liberal criticism, which obliges conservatives to consider their own existence as problematic. That may be true. But according to Mannheim's own definition the "counter-utopia" is not a genuine utopia, since its function is not to "transcend reality" but to maintain the fundamental illusion of conservative ideology — that of a congruence between consciousness and being (Seinskongruenz). The conservative utopia is in Mannheim's view not only bearer of a specific form of false consciouness but it is also a bastardized concept that belongs simultaneously to the field of ideology and of utopia. The same holds true a fortiori for the so-called reactionary utopia.[16]

Mannheim's critical analysis of chiliastic (Anabaptist) utopia is interesting for a different reason. It is probably one of the first attempts at a sociological analysis of the experience of time; in this respect it prefigured the latter studies of G. Gurvitch.[17]

"The chiliastic consciousness has . . . no sense for the process of becoming; it was sensitive only to the abrupt moment, the present pregnant with meaning. The form of consciousness which remains on the Chiliastic level neither knows nor recognizes . . . either a road that leads to a goal or a process of development — it knows only the tide and ebb of time."[18]

This chiliastic notion of time has undeniably some schizophrenic features. The notion of an absolute present, the downfall of temporalisation and the obsession with the immediate, are reminiscent of the schizophrenic experience of time described, among others, by Binswanger, Minkowski, and Honorio Delgado.[19] Curiously in analyzing the temporality of Anabaptist consciousness Mannheim was once again confronted with the traditional notion of utopia, as if he were forced by a logical necessity to return to that which he was trying to avoid. He also put his finger on one of the dominant mechanisms of the process of the ideologization of orthodox Marxism. Once more Mannheim foreshadows Orwell.

Mannheim's purpose when elaborating his typology of ideology was, as we have seen above, to recuperate the concept of ideology for scientific politics, after having discarded elements of Manichean egocentricity. For the special and particular ("polemical") concept of ideology the basis of ideologization is deliberate mystification; now the mystifier is, in principle, the opponent. For the total and general ("structural") concept, ideologization is tantamount to a "socially determined" (*seinsgebunden*) distortion of the logical framework of political thought. Now since no political thought is admittedly exempt from social influence, this concept does not concede a privileged position to the "ingroup" and escapes the trap of political egocentricity.

The introduction of the concept of "transcendence of the social being" (*Seinstranszendenz*) into the critique of utopian consciousness, conveys the same concern. The classic concept of utopia (an unattainable social project) is potentially a source of political egocentricity; it is generally the "dereistic" desire of the opponent or at least of a rival that is branded as utopian. The concept of *Seinstranszendenz* is supposed to perform here the same function as the total and general concept of ideology: to have the way for a scientific approach to the problem after eliminating the trap of egocentricity that impends over committed political thinking.

The two approaches are not equally valid from a scientific point of view. Apart from a few details Mannheim's theory of ideology is certainly a valuable contribution to this problem. The same cannot be said of his analysis of utopian consciousness, which leads to such dubious concepts as that of conservative utopia. It is a strange experience to read Ruyer's book right after Mannheim's, you feel that you have regained terra firma.

Mannheim had foreseen the withering away of the utopian dimension of political programs, but he was by no means enthusiastic about this perspective. "Thus we approach a situation in which the utopian element, through its many divergent forms, has completely (in politics at least) annihilated itself. . . .  The ultimate triumph of freedom will be a dry one").[20] When political parties enter parliament, the utopian side of their programs is pushed into the background and priority is given to practical routine concerns. The viewpoint of dialectical totality survives at the two extremes of the political gamut: in the neo-Marxism of Lukàcs and in the "universalism" of Othmar Spann. Between those extremes, the central area aspires to nothing more than devoting itself to overspecialized activities with no individuality or local color.[21] American social thought, harmonized with capitalist reality, serves as a model, and a sociology indifferent to historical time takes shape in the United States. For Mannheim, utopia is a "historiogenic" factor, instrumental in the production of dialectical political awareness; Raymond Ruyer made in his book, *L'Utopie et les utopies*, a diametrically opposed statement. Would Mannheim sign his name to the above-quoted passage in 1990? I wonder. When *Ideologie und Utopie* was published, the utopian element of political programs seemed doomed to die away. Since 1929, utopia has made some dramatic reappearances on the political scene, and not always for the good. A "dry" victory of freedom is preferable to wet slavery in the rice fields of Cambodia.

## Notes

1. (Paris: P.U.F., 1950). Mannheim's concept of utopia is a mirror image of R. Ruyer's. According to Mannheim, utopia helps to accelerate history; it is therefore a bad sign when it is missing from politics. In Ruyer's view, utopism arises from psychologically borderline people who escape into an imaginary (not to say hallucinatory) historicity and sociality. Utopian consciousness as described by R. Ruyer has a typically schizophrenic structure: that is why it can be interpreted as a form of false consciousness.

   In a seminar on "Utopian Discourse" held in Cerisy-la-Salle in August 1975, I proposed a typology distinguishing between Mannheim's "surrealist" conception of utopia and Ruyer's "subrealist" conception. Other participants spoke of "Dionysian" and "Apollonian" conceptions, which basically amounts to the same thing. The term "surrealist" seems the best able to recreate the meaning of Mannheim's German expressions *seinstranszendent* and *wirklichkeitssprengend;* it is preferable to *"situationellement transcendant,"* which is a mistranslation, and *"transcendant par rapport à l'être,"* which is unwieldy. It is not disturbing that the term coincides with the name of a de-mystifying politico-literary movement, since that indirectly recalls the issue of political mystification, i.e. of false consciousness. (See Maurice de Gandillac, *Le Discours Utopique* (minutes of the Cerisy seminar), Paris, 10/18, 1978, 38 and 48.

2. The German expression *Seinstranszendent* refers to the ambition of an individual or a collectivity (a social class or an ethnic minority) to "break the bonds of the existing order." The subversive overtone of the original term is completely occulted in the translation, and in the French translation ("situationnellement transcendant") even more than in the English one.

3. This passage, which is essential for understanding Mannheim, is on p. 53 of the 1965 edition and is usually quoted in this essay, and on p. 7 of the 1929 edition. It is hard to say whether the omission was consented to by Mannheim. In any case, no matter what its cause may be, it hinders a full understanding of Mannheim's message.

4. In the review *L'Homme et la Société*, no. 11 (1969).

5. Ernst Bloch, *Freiheit und Ordnung. Abriss der Sozial-Utopien* (New York: Aurora Verlag, 1946), 160–75.

6. The "social project" of the Khmers Rouges in Cambodia featured many "Ruyerian" and "Orwellian" traits such as the abolition of money and *prohibition of wearing glasses* (in the name of egalitarianism, no doubt). This last point is typical: abstract *social* egalitarianism legitimates *natural* inequality among those with normal eyesight and the short-sighted or far-sighted who are no longer able to compensate for the inequality. See Pin Yathay, *L'utopie meurtrière* (Paris: Ed. Famot, 1980), vol. 1, 71.

7. Reprinted in *Idéologies* (Paris: Anthropos, 1974).

8. Pierre Ansart, *Les ideologies politiques* (Paris: P.U.F., 1974), 85–6.

9. F. Laplantine, *Les trois voix de l'imaginaire* (Paris: Ed. Universitaires, 1974), 255–56.

10. See J. Gabel, "Délire politique chez un paranoïde," *L'Evolution psychiatrique,* 1952, reprinted in *Ideologies* (1974), 314–24 under the new title: "Rêveries utopiques chez un schizophrène."

11. R. Ruyer *L'Utopie* 41, 70, 98, 107, 227 ff.

12. A. Kolnai "L'Utopie réactionnaire," *Cité Libre Montréal,* Nov. 1955.

13. Mannheim, *Ideology and Utopia* (London: Routledge & Kegan, 1948) 209 (see German edition, 1965, 201–02).

14. Mannheim, *Ideology and Utopia*, 173; German edition, 1965, 169.

15. Mannheim, *Ideology and Utopia*, 206; German edition, 1965, 199.

16. Subversive utopias promote a belief in the impossible; reactionary utopias impose a belief in lies" (Kolnai, *"L'Utopie réactionnaire,"* 84). In all probability, that is a question of ideology rather than one of utopia.

And the fascist utopia? The human stud-farms *(Lebensborn)* dreamed up by Himmler's morbid imagination might be the model for it. But that form of utopia is more closely related to Fourier's paranoid phantasms than to a political project worthy of the name.

17. G. Gurvitch, "Structures sociales et multiplicité des temps," *Cahiers de l'Institut des Sciences economiques appliqués* n. 99 (1960).

18. Mannheim, *Ideology and Utopia*, 202; German edition, 1965, 195.

19. According to Honorio Delgado the schizophrenic time structure is characterized by "retrospective invalidation of historical data" (*invalidacion de lo acaecido*) and by the reification of time. This is exactly the utopico-ideological time structure of *1984*. See H. Delgado, "Anormalidades de la conciencia del tiempo," *Revista de Psiquiatria y de Psicologia de Europa y America Latina* n. 1 (1953).

20. Mannheim, *Ideology and Utopia*, 225.

21. Ibid., 227. The English translation of this passage is incomplete. See *Ideologie und Utopie* (German edition 1965), 217–18.

# 9

# Critique of Mannheim's Sociology of Knowledge

Mannheim became the main representative — if not the founder — of sociology of knowledge almost through a misunderstanding. He was not the inventor of that term, which was first used in 1909 by a long-forgotten German philosopher, Wilhelm Jerusalem.[1] Moreover, the researches of the French sociological school, such as the sociological deduction of the categories of thought by Durkheim, the study by Mauss and Beuchat on seasonal variations of the Eskimo, as well as the analysis of the influence of the social context on individual and collective forms of memory by Maurice Halbwachs, are authentic and pertinent studies in the sociology of knowledge and predate those by Mannheim.

*Ideology and Utopia* and the essay on German conservative thought (*Das konservative Denken*) are brilliant essays of political sociology. They have however little to do with sociology of knowledge in the strict sense of this term. The same holds true for a polemical article against Max Scheler which — despite its title — is a plea for historicism rather than a study in the sociology of knowledge.[2] In fact, only three of his works clearly belong to the tradition of the sociology of knowledge but they are hardly among Mannheim's best scientific achievements.[3] Mannheim offers programs, clarifies theoretical issues, "situates" the sociology of knowledge, and sometimes contributes practical suggestions to the debate. He is the "public relations man" of the sociology of knowledge rather than a genuine theorist of this discipline; he passionately defends it but rarely applies it.

An usurped title—despite the good faith of the usurper—is not without its dangers. "Ill begotten goods do no good" as the saying goes. I have tried to show that the work of Mannheim, critical theorist of the ideological phenomenon, remains unmatched. Yet the shortcomings of his sociology of knowledge and among others, his aversion to empirical research, have not escaped the attention of critical readers such as Raymond Aron.[4] Mannheim is frequently judged by the shortcomings of one problematic chapter of his work, and this judgement while partially justified, was unduly extrapolated to his entire work. The brilliant theorist of the ideology is so overshadowed by an ordinary sociologist of knowledge. Mannheim was one of the brightest stars in the academic scene of Weimar Germany, and his influence on Anglo-Saxon intellectual life has been considerable. In France his writings met with a poor response. This failure is in my view due to the distortion of his work by his opponents, by his supporters, and, in the final analysis, by Mannheim himself. Mannheim was nominated founder of the sociology of knowledge in much the same way as Sancho Panza was appointed as governor of an island. More naive than the legendary squire, Mannheim held fast to this title, therefore exposing himself to justifiable criticism. A man who has both a ragged outfit and an elegant suit and who insists on wearing the former has only himself to blame if he is taken for a bum.

Mannheim's sociology of knowledge was marked by the ball and chain he had to drag around: the exclusion of exact sciences from its sphere of validity and its lack of differentiation between facts of consciousness and facts of knowledge. Mannheim does not reject the traditional Marxist assumption of the falseness of bourgeois consciousness, but since the political consciousness of the working class can itself fall into the trap of ideologization, he needs an Archimedean point for his *Ideologiekritik*. We have seen above that this Archimedean point is in his view the rootless Intelligentsia whose capacity to synthetise partial political perspectives is seen as a source of dialectical and historicist awareness.

Now once such a dynamic synthesis has been achieved, the conditions of the emergence of the sociology of knowledge are supposed to be realized. Mannheim's formulation is unambiguous: "With the emergence of the general formulation of the total conception of ideology, the simple theory of ideology develops into the sociology of knowledge."[5] We are thus transferred from the sphere of consciousness to that of knowledge as if by magic. According to V.G. Hinshaw the source of confusion in Mannheim's approach is "his inability to distinguish between the cognitive and noncognitive aspects" of that which is commonly called knowledge, and "if the sociology of knowledge is the direct and immediate heir to the general theory of total ideology, it is inextricably mixed up with unscientific emotional elements."[6]

By excluding the exact sciences from the sphere of the sociology of knowledge, Mannheim contributed to reducing confusion, but it was at a high price. The mutual neutralisation of opposed forms of false consciousness is supposed to give birth—illegitimately in my view—to a sociology of knowledge whose task is no longer unmasking, but functionalization. Mannheim attempted to still the doubts raised by the mysterious passage quoted above by excluding from the sphere of the sociology of knowledge all knowledge other than political knowledge and its derivatives, that is, the field of knowledge that is most inextricably tied up with facts of consciousness.[7] J. J. Maquet is utterly right in blaming Mannheim for his illegitimate generalization of lessons drawn from the analysis of a different and specific domain. Mannheim's painstaking attempt to bridge the gap between the critical sociology of ideologies and the sociology of knowledge appears as an illusion.[8] Mannheim's situation in this question is reminiscent of that of an illegal border-crosser who is apprehended by the frontier-guards and is brought back to his point of departure.

It appears now clearly why Mannheim's sociology of knowledge was unable to go beyond the stage of generalities. His definition of the sociology of knowledge (*Wissenssoziologie*) is somewhat arbitrary; the German term *Wissen* never did refer exclusively to political or social knowledge. His polemic against Scheler is most certainly a brilliant performance but, in spite of its title, it is more relevant to the critique of ideology than to the sociology of knowledge.[9]

Consequently Mannheim failed to recognize the importance of the social determination of exact science. It seems that he never freed himself from the apprehension that the validity of the achievements of exact science could be challenged if "placed in historical perspective." Now the genuine adventure of the sociology of knowledge begins at the very point where Mannheim left it off: the issue of the social determination of science. Many issues are raised: scientific false consciosusness in its relationsship to epistemology,[10] the epistemological and gnoseo-sociological role of the dialectic, the problem of selective or constitutive action of the social context (Grünwald). Since Mannheim ignored such problems there is no reason to analyze them in this particular study, which is devoted to his work and not to specific problems in the sociology of knowledge. However the mere enumeration of these issues suffices to show that Mannheim is by no means a typical representative of the sociology of knowledge. The center of gravity of his scientific achievement is located elsewhere.

My purpose in this chapter is to oppose to the conventional image of "Mannheim sociologist of knowledge" that of "Mannheim critical theorist of the problem of political alienation" (i.e. of the ideology). Things are of course not so simple in reality. Mannheim's writings, especially those of his early period, often inextricably intermix *Ideologiekritik* and *Wissenssoziologie*. It must be clearly pointed out that Mannheim saw himself first and foremost as a sociologist of knowledge. Nevertheless the "idealtype" of his thought elaborated from his writings on ideology is both more coherent and more up to date than the "idealtype" resulting exclusively from his texts of sociology of knowledge.

This distinction between *relativism* and *relationism* and the polemic against Scheler's "metectic" concept of the sociology of knowledge offer some good arguments in favor of our initial hypothesis. Mannheim opposes "vulgar relativism," ("Man is the measure of all things") a socio-historical *relationism* supported by references to the theory of relativity[11] and to the Viennese school of epistemology. "An indication of the conditions under which a proposition is true is consubstantial to its meaning."[12] This statement by Moritz Schlick, a well-known member of the Viennese school, holds a fortiori true for human sciences such as history and politics. It is impossible to establish with absolute certitude that economic rivalry between Germany and Great Britain was the main cause of World War I. It is, on the other hand, quite permissible to assert that in the historical perspective of a German nationalist, this rivalry appears as the principal cause of the conflict. Mannheim's relationist principle — akin to Max Weber's *Wertbeziehung* — is basically an effort to transcend the visceral egocentricity of "pre-scientific" political consciousness. Mannheim's purpose was to replace "relativism" that borders on nihilism with a principle of mutual understanding and conciliation. Consider, though, that these views were formulated before 1933. The emergence of Hitlerism on the scene of history was for the theorist of the synthesis of different perspectives tantamount to a serious moral and intellectual challenge.

The importance of this differentiation was underestimated by some Marxists but also by some "pure" sociologists of knowledge, little interested in the autonomous problem of ideology. According to Georg Lukàcs, "the difference between relativism and relationism is about the same as that between the yellow and green devil."[13] Hinshaw, Ernest Grünwald, and Werner Stark express similar reservations in less diabolical terms, and claim that this differentiation between relativism and relationism is nothing but a simple verbal artifice in order to keep the sociology of knowledge from paying its due to scepticism.[14]

Of course it is not at all so, but the scientific meaning of this differentiation is located outside the domain of the sociology of knowledge. The concept of relation contributes an important factor of "de-reification" to the debate. According to Lukàcs, reification is tantamount to a phenomenon of "phantom-like objectiveness" (*gespänstige Gegenständlichkeit*) that covers up the relational essence of human reality. Reification of relational facts has been pointed out in the language of politics[15] and even in schizophrenia.[16] Now, taking into account the fact that alienation involves frequently the reification of relational facts, we may infer that conversely relationism may be an instrument of de-alienation. The same does not hold true for relativism. With all the respect due to Lukàcs, I see here a more significant difference than that which exists between devils of different coloration (why not "Brown devil versus red devil?"). Mannheim's distinction remains valid, but its essential meaning falls outside the domain of the sociology of knowledge proper.

A similar demonstration could be attempted concerning the objective significance of the polemic against Scheler's "metectic" sociology of knowledge (metexis =participation). This term was coined by Werner Stark who opposes the "metectic" sociology of knowledge to its "pragmatic" variety represented by authors such as Auguste Comte, Emile Durkheim, and Mannheim.[17] According to the pragmatic conception, truth is an attribute of existence rather than of discourse.[18] It should be added that the term "existence" means *social* existence under the signature of Durkheim and *historical* existence in the work of Mannheim. Durkheim "sociologizes" the philosophy while Mannheim "historicizes" it;[19] their common rejection of all kinds of essentialism sets them apart from Max Scheler. However solely from the viewpoint of the sociology of knowledge, this debate might seem to be merely a matter of terminology. Georg Gurvitch[20] points out that the difference between these two authors affects their philosophical credo rather than their sociological procedure as such.[21] Werner Stark, who sees this debate exclusively through the eyes of a sociologist of knowledge, fails to perceive its objective meaning and remarks that "metectic theory is bad in practice, even though it may be good in principle."[22] That is, no doubt, a little simplistic.

In fact the historical significance of the Mannheim-Scheler debate is a dramatic one. Once again it is beyond the reach of the sociology of knowledge and it transcended to some extent the awareness of its protagonists. Behind Scheler's inoffensive sociological platonism the historicist critique reached a far more important target. Political ideologies "platonize" in their own way, not by striving for "essences" outside of space and time but by *essentializing their own points of view*[23] which are raised to the level of a "false absolute."[24] This is particularly symptomatic of a totalitarian mentality which interprets reality according to its own conceptual system in which "essences" extracted by egocentrical techniques are illegitimately given a privileged *logical* position.[25] This calls to mind the whole ideological context opposed objectively by Mannheim's historicist polemic. A jobless German who might have said in 1933 "I am poverty stricken but my essence is that of a superior race" would make a sort of compensatory metexis (with all due respect to Scheler). The objective significance of the debate concerns the problem of alienation rather than the sociology of knowledge. Seen solely in the context of the latter, the debate loses an essential dimension and may appear to be a mere scholastic quarrel.

This phase of Mannheim's work must be seen in its original social context to be fully understood: Germany's Weimar Republic of which France's Fourth Republic was a sort of attenuated historical replica without the harsh but stimulating ambience characteristic of Germany at this time. Compact and complete *Weltanschauungen* (some later to become totalitarian) clashed in a furious effort of unmasking.[26] Nothing is more characteristic of the ideological climate of that epoch — an extremely attractive one for all its harshness — than the title of Paul Szende's essay: *Mystification and demystification; the struggle of ideologies throughout History.*

The terrible memory of postwar inflation, the public need to exorcize the country of its responsibility for the war, and the "shame of defeat" led to a doubly paradoxical result. The nihilism of a fraction of the youth reflected the collapse of values, while another part of the public tried to block out the precariousness of values by clinging to a cult of reified and supra-historical "values" (racism). Finally the contrast between the deceptive nature of the social reality and the attractiveness of utopian projects of every kind prepared public opinion to accept Manichean forms of political consciousness such as Hitlerism and Stalinism.

In the midst of these powerful ideological currents in competition for the control of German political consciousness, the position of Mannheim, an academic of Jewish origin and German by naturalization, was very typically "freischwebend." The logic inherent to this position steered him towards a non-ideological perception of the political debate in Weimar Germany and the validity of this awareness was naturally not limited to the "hic et nunc." It is by no means fortuitous that nearly all of Mannheim's polemical writings of this time (those against Max Scheler as well as those directed against sectarian Marxists) concern rudimentary forms of false consciousness that were to crystallize later on.

In the sociology of knowledge Mannheim was first and foremost a "great awakener of ideas."[27] His importance lies not so much in his own contribution—which is modest and more theoretical than practical—but rather in the influence he managed to exert. In doing so he indirectly did an unexpected service to French sociology. He drew the attention of American sociologists to the sociology of knowledge. Once this latter had become a recognized speciality, American sociologists, better connoisseurs of French scientific literature than their German colleagues, were quick to point out that it was Durkheim's school rather than Mannheim that deserved credit for having established the sociology of knowledge as has clearly been shown by Robert K. Merton.[28]

According to Raymond Aron, Mannheim's sociology of knowledge, "contributed no new theory of the relation subject-object, nor any original analysis of the conditions of truth, nor even an analysis of positive science."[29] This statement is confirmed by the fact that preoccupations in the sociology of knowledge are virtually absent in the writings of his final (Anglo-Saxon) period.

My own approach to this problem has led to the same result, but in my view Aron's criticism is relevant only to the *epistemological* form of the sociology of knowledge represented by Mannheim.[30] Its *substantive* variety illustrated by authors such as Hinshaw and Stark, whose main reference is Scheler rather than Mannheim, poses a different problem that does not concern us here. By holding tight to his epistemological aspirations, Mannheim cut himself off from an "analysis of positive science." But the most tangible conclusion we can arrive at is that certain of his findings, of little interest to sociologists of knowledge, remain significant in the context of his theory of ideology. Once more this latter appears as the chapter of Mannheim's work destined to survive.

## Notes

1. W. Jerusalem, "Die soziologische Bedingtheit des Denkens und der Denkformen, in Max Scheler," *Versuche zu einer Soziologie des Wissens*, München-Leipzig, Duncker und Humblot Verl., 1924, 182–207.
2. Mannheim, "Das Problem einer Soziologie des Wissens," *Archiv für Sozialwissenschaft und Sozialpolitik*, 1925, reprinted in *Wissenssoziologie* (Berlin: Luchterhand Verl, 1964), 308–87.
3. It is a question of the following articles by Mannheim: "Ideologische und Soziologische Betrachtung der geistigen Gebilde," *Jahrbuch für Soziologie*, Karlsruhe, 1926; "Preliminary approach to the Problem," introduction to the English edition of *d'Idéologie und Utopie* et *Wissenssoziologie* in *Handwörterbuch für Soziologie* by A. Vierkandt. This last text is also featured in the English translation of *Ideology and Utopia*.
4. See, inter alia, G. Gurvitch, "Le problème de la sociologie de la connaissance," *Revue Philosophique*, 1958–59, and R. Aron, *La Sociologie Allemande Contemporaine*.
5. *Ideologie und Utopie*, 1965, 70; French translation, 1956, 75.
6. V.G. Hinshaw, "The Epistemological Relevance of Mannheim's Sociology of Knowledge," *The Journal of Philosophy*, XL, no. 3 (February 1943): 69.
7. "An inseparable admixture of factionary bias and cognitive facts," Hinshaw, "Epistemological Relevance," 69.
8. Jacques Maquet, *Sociologie de la connaissance, sa structure et ses rapports avec la philosophie de la connaissance. Etude critique des systèmes de Karl Mannheim et de Pitirim A. Sorokine* (Louvain: E. Nauwelaerts, 1949).

9. In his quoted article, "Das Problem einer Soziologie des Wissens," a very brilliant article which, however, is concerned with everything but the sociology of knowledge.

10. Regarding the problem of false consciousness in the sciences, see G. Canguilhem, *Idéologie et rationalité dans l'histoire des sciences de la vie* (Paris: Vrin, 1977), and my article "Une pensée non-idéologique est-elle possible" in Jean Duvignaud, *Sociologie de la connaissance* (Paris: Payot, 1979), 13-22.

11. Remember that Paul Szende, Mannheim's forerunner in the field of the critique of ideology, was highly interested in Einsteinian relativity.

12. Moritz Schlick, *Les énoncés scientifiques et la réalité du monde extérieur* (Paris: Hermann, 1934), 24.

13. Lukàcs, *Die Zerstörung der Vernunft* (Berlin, 1955), 500.

14. E. Grunwald, *Das Problem der Soziologie des Wissens* (Leipzig: Braumüller Verl. 1934), 230; W. Stark, *The Sociology of Knowledge. An essay in aid of a deeper understanding of the history of ideas* (Glencoe, Ill.: Free Press, 1958), 339; and Hinshaw, Epistemological Relevance, 61.

15. Sociocentric expressions like "anti-communist," "anti-party," or "un-American," reify the relationships they describe. This phenomenon was particularly intense in Stalinist ideology.

16. Some psychoanalysts (Katan, Racamier, Roheim) have shown the existence of authentic phenomena of reification (without using the term) in the language of schizophrenics.

17. W. Stark, *Sociology of Knowledge*, 324, 328.

18. "Truth . . . is an attribute of existence rather than of discourse." Ibid., 327.

19. Cf. the sociological deduction of categories in *Les Formes élémentaires de la vie religieuse* by Durkheim.

20. G. Gurvitch, *problème de la sociologie,* 448.

21. "For us the eyes of God contemplate History, which implies that History is given a meaning; as for Scheler, he came to postulate that he himself contemplated History with the eyes of God," Mannheim, *Das Problem einer Soziologie des Wissens,* p. 637.

22. "Metectic theory is bad in practice, even if it be good in principle." W. Stark, *Sociology of Knowledge*, 341.

23. Existentialism is frequently placed in opposition to essentialism (see P. Foulquié: *L'existentialisme* (Paris: P.U.F. 1949). In my view, existentialism is more opposed to the reified pseudo-essentialism of totalitarian ideologies since existentialism, like surrealism, is a doctrine of de-alienation.

24. The importance of "false absolutes" in the psycho-sociology of the Hitler

movement has been clearly pointed out by Wilfried Daim in *Umwertung der Psychoanalyse* (Vienna, 1951).

25. Stalinism was almost a grotesque form of this "refusal to place one's own point of view in perspective" combined with "justificatory essentialism" and "false identifications."

26. This "will to unmask at any price," one of the most typical traits of Weimar intellectual life, also had its drawbacks. Hitlerism was "functionalized" by Marxists, as a last attempt to save the capitalist system, which covered up its independent meaning pointed out later by Bruno Rizzi in *Bureaucratisation du Monde* (1939) and by James Burnham in *The Managerial Revolution* (1941).

27. G. Gurvitch, *Le problème de la sociologie,* 466 note. Bestowed by G. Gurvitch, an exacting judge in the field, it is a fine title.

28. See Robert K. Merton, "The Sociology of Knowledge" in *Twentieth Century Sociology* (New York: Philosophical Library, 1945), and "Karl Mannheim and the Sociology of Knowledge," *Journal of Liberal Religion,* Chicago, 1941. In his quoted study W. Jerusalem fully acknowledges the rights to priority of Durkheim's school in this area. E. Grunwald, *Problem der Soziologie,* 16 is more reserved.

29. R. Aron, *La sociologie allemande contemporaine* (Paris: P.U.F., 1950), 10.

30. The so-called substantive conception considers sociologists of knowledge to be "behavior scientists" (Hinshaw, *"Epistemological Relevance,"* 70) who are not interested in the problem of the *validity* of theories. This attitude makes it easier to create a sociology of *scientific knowledge.* In fact, once it assumed that sociological determination has no influence on the validity of statements, there is no reason to reject the idea of a sociological determination of science considered as a *superstructure* but not necessarily as an *ideology.* That is the interpretation of the role of the sociology of knowledge held by authors such as Scheler, Hinshaw, and Stark. Concerning Scheler, see H. Becker and H.O. Dahlke "Max Scheler's Sociology of Knowledge" in P*hilosophy and Phenomenological Research,* 1941–42, 310–22.

Mannheim took a different path. In his view, the sociology of knowledge, deeply interested in the sociological dimension of the *validity* of statements, plays the role of something like an *ancilla epistemologiae.* But his orientation bore only bitter fruit. According to Hinshaw, "Mannheim's confusion in trying to develop an epistemological sociology of knowledge lies precisely in his partial failure both to distinguish cognitive from non cognitive aspects of 'knowledge' as well as to realise the vitiating influence of just this evaluative component in the 'knowledge' of any period" (*"Epistemological Relevance,"* 70), and the same author added with a touch of cruel irony: "Mannheim is outrunning his functions as sociologist of knowledge and has become an incompetent epistemologist" (Ibid., 67).

In fact this is perhaps even more serious, since Mannheim, the author of an epistemological thesis, could not be accused of genuine incompetence in this area. If his "epistemological" sociology of knowledge gives rather disappointing results, it is because it could not do any better because of its very nature.

# 10

## Socially Determined Thought and Historical Materialism: Mannheim and Marxism

The interpretation by Mannheim of historical materialism is in direct line with his theory of ideology. With his notion of *Seinsgebundenheit des Denkens*, Mannheim added his own personal form of historical "materialism," in which, despite the assertions of Lukàcs,[1] the economic element is not absent but given a lesser part to play than the notion of dialectical totality which is raised to the status of a sociological category. Kurt Lenk's formula is straight to the point but causes difficulty in translation: Mannheim aims at "eine Funktionalisierung geistiger Gehalte auf die dahinter stehende soziale *Seinstotalität*.[2] G. Gurvitch, for his part, considers that the theory of "thought linked to the social level" implies a reciprocal conditioning of knowledge by social situations and consequently of social situations by knowledge" and furthermore points out that "as Mannheim's sociology of knowledge enters into greater detail, Marxist elements grow less important . . ."[3] Mannheim, in his role as a sociologist of knowledge, takes his distance with regard to Marxism, but his moving away is in a *dialectical* direction. Such "dialectization" is apparent on two levels: 1) that of totality (Lenk); and that of 2) the dialectical interaction of knowledge and being (Gurvitch).

The significance of such an orientation cannot be minimized. Within the framework of Marxist theory, both materialist and dialectical components are not always in harmony; their coexistence has always been

103

in juxtaposition rather than in synthesis. According to Robert Meigniez's witty formulation Marxism involves two different doctrines: a more or less "dialectical" materialism and a more or less "materialistic" dialectic. Russian Marxism of the Stalinist era is a genuine epitome of the first tendency; that of G. Lukàcs and his followers (such as among others L. Goldmann and Mannheim himself) well illustrates the second. The hostility of Stalinism toward dialectics is a well-known fact in the history of ideologies: it was pointed out as early as 1923 by Karl Korsch in his classic work, *Marsixmus and Philosophie* and later on by theorists such as Leo Kofler and the present author.[4] The dualistic conception of ideology as elaborated by Mannheim, corresponds to this fundamental dualism of Marxist theory. The partial (polemical) conception of ideology is the natural corollary of a materialist interpretation of Marxism perceived as being first and foremost an economic determinism that considers class interest as the "primum movens" of the process of ideologization. Conversely the "total" (structural) conception of the ideloogy is corollary to a dialectical rather than materialist perception of Marxism ("Hungaro-Marxism" in the terminology coined by the present author) since it considers dedialectization as the essential element of ideologization. When this process of dedialectization affects the "dialectical totality" that constitutes society, ideologization appears in the form of "society-blindness."[5] The whole Stalinist ideological stands, which in the field of philosophy opted for materialism as against dialectics, and, in sociology for determinism as against *Seinsgebundenheit*, is here; in its theory of consciousness opting for "conscience as reflection" rather than "conscience as a conquest" (Lukàcs) and in its theory of ideology finally it preferred partial (polemical) conception to total (structural) one, and thus constituted in terms of sociology of knowledge, a coherent whole and that coherence throws much light on many points of detail. This does not become truly apparent, nevertheless, until considered in the light of Mannheim's differentiation of the concept of ideology whose practical usefulness can then be perceived.

We can well understand the severity of orthodox Marxist criticism. In the appendix to his work *Marxizmus és Logika* (*Marxism & Logic*) Fogarasi blames his ex-countryman, Mannheim for having substituted the precision of Marx's formulation with a "vague obscure and imprecise category."[6] According to Fogarasi, Marx never spoke of "socially bound thought" (*Seinsgebundenes Denken*) but of "socially determined consciousness," which is of course not the same thing. Leaving aside for the moment the implied criticism of employing the concepts "consciousness" and "thought" interchangeably, it must be said against the charge that Mannheim is not the only guilty party. As for criticising a lack of precision, some explanation is required: precision is not always to be counted an asset in doctrinal conception; it may even prove a weakness if it restricts the scope of application. Dogmatic Marxism tends to interpret the historical past in the exclusive terms of economic determinism. Its understanding of contemporary political events is shot through with *idealistic* elements representing the party's role as a demiurge and—in its most extreme form—by personality cult. Sidney Hook observes that "the importance granted to *conscious* action by the political party, far from representinng an idealistic deviation from Marxism, is really at the core of Marx's revolutionary position."[7]

As it turned out later, the "personality cult" symptomatic of a genuinely idealist conception of history, was implicit in the Leninist conception of the historical role of the party. The same holds true for the "history making" ("historiogène") role ascribed in a different political context, to Mao's *thought*. This clearly illustrates that there was question from the very outset of idealist deviation. According to Calvez, "Stalin saw himself led to insist not only on the role of institutions, the Party and the Soviet State, but also on that of *ideas* and theories."[8]

Contemporary events do not exist outside history. Lukàcs, rightly, denounced the inability of bourgeois thinkers and historians to understand contemporary events in world history as historical but his criticism is also implicitly directed at the historical sensitivity of orthodox Marxism.[9] By claiming the unconditional validity of the materialistic principle *in theory*, orthodox Marxism is condemned to gloss over that principle when interpreting contemporary political events; orthodox Marxist historical theory sets out claims of being both materialist and dialectic, but its practical application to contemporary events is, on the contrary, idealist and Manichean. It is an outstanding example of the phenomenon that Mannheim designated *split consciousness*. It is not convenient to intransigently explain the historical past according to one principle and contemporary events to one that is diametrically opposed; the present is historical, and only an egocentrism of the present (presento-centrism) can give substance to the illusion that it is structurally different from the past. By making historical materialism more flexible and dialectic, Mannheim's procedure tried to narrow the gap. Yet again, his interpretation is an example of what could be called "thinking against," a form of ideologization of historical sensitivity. Historicism — in just the same way as with Personalism, according to J. Lacroix — is basically an "anti-ideology" in Mannheim's writings.[10]

Mannheim's attenuation of the severity of Marxist determinism has its drawbacks, however. Many critics have complained that Mannheim's terms are rather imprecise. Merton and Maquet[11] basically repeat the orthodox Marxist attack on Mannheim (by Fogarasi), but they base their criticisms on a rather comprehensive list of Mannheim's expressions designating the relations between consciousness and being. Note that Merton's list is in English and Maquet's in French, whereas the most often-quoted work was written in German. An analysis of the original texts does indeed show a certain amount of terminological inconsistency, but to a lesser extent.

The following list is Merton's to which the original passages have been added.[12]

"...being in accord with the needs of time" in the original text: "...als zeitgemässe gehalten."[13]

"...causal determinants..." "...mit einer bestimmten kausalen Zwangsläufgkeit..."[14]

"... a given set of concepts... bound up with and growing out of a certain social reality..." "... die soziale Gebundenheit einer Kategorialapparatur gerade durch diese vitale Bindung..."[15]

"When the social situation changes, the system of norms to which it had previously given birth ceases to be in harmony with it ..." " ... Verschiebt sich das Sein so entfremdet sich ihm auch das früher von ihm "gezeugte" Normsystem..."[16]

"The intellectualistic conception of science, underlying positivism, is itself rooted in a definite Weltanschauung and has progressed in close connection with definite political interests." " ... dass jenes intellektualistische Wissenschaftsbild, das dem Positivismus zugrunde liegt, selbst in einer Weltanschauung wurzelt und mit bestimmten politischen Wollungen eng verknüpft sich durchgesetzt hat."[17]

*"Socially, this intellectualistic outlook had its basis in a middle stratum, in the bourgeoisie and in the intellectual class. This outlook, in accordance with the structural relationship of the group representing it, pursued a dynamic middlecourse between the vitality, ecstasy and vindictiveness of oppressed strata and the immediate concreteness of a feudal ruling class whose aspirations were in complete congruence with the then existing reality." "Sozial wurde das ideenhafte Bewusstsein getragen von einer mittleren Schicht, vom Bürgertum und von der Intelligenz. Dieser Strukturlage entsprechend hielt es die strebend dynamische Mitte zwischen der sinnlichen Vitalität, Ekstase, Rachelust unterdruckter Schichten und der unvermittelten Konkretheit einer in unproblematischcr Koinzidenz mit der damaligen Wirklichkeit sich befindenden feudal herrschenden Schicht."[18]*

*"Ideas, forms of thought and psychic energies persist and are transformed in close conjunction with social forces. It is never by accident that they appear at given moments in the social process." "Gehalte, Denkformen, seelische Energien erhalten und transformieren sich im Bündnis mit sozialen Kräften und treten niemals zufällig an bestimmten Orten im sozialen Geschehen auf."[19]*

A close analysis of the original texts clearly shows that there is less terminological inconsistency in German than in the translation. Indeed, there is inconsistency, *but this is not of necessity an avowal of weakness.* The English translators remark: "The German expression *Seinsverbundenes Wissen* conveys a meaning which leaves the exact nature of determinism open" (English translation, 1948, 239). It is not an impractical thesis that Marxist scholars leave with a dismissive nod of the head at the door of their laboratories or hospital wards, but it is a working principle. An investigation of most classical Marxist writers (including Marx himself) might well produce the same results. Robert K. Merton sees such terminological inconsistency to be a portent of a "fundamental indecision," but is this not rather the scholar's respect for the fundamental variety of reality? The term, *Entsprechung,* (correspondence) so dear to Mannheim, is above all a sign of prudence that is quite justifiable. Its use is perhaps a way of "thinking against" the dogmatism of vulgar Marxism.

In spite of the assertions of Lukàcs, Mannheim had no desire to eliminate the economic factor of causal mechanisms from the determination of the historical process; he merely restricted its validity to the capitalist era. Lukàcs had less right than any other to censure this procedure, for Mannheim closely follows certain developments in his

*History and Class Consciousness* in that respect, so much so that his originality could well have been called into question. The chapter "The Change in the Function of Historical Materialism"[20] should be kept in mind: it is not futile to point out that this very chapter reproduces a lecture given by Lukàcs when he was a member of the Béla Kun-Garbai regime[21] — that is probably one of the hidden reasons for the book's disfavor. It remains a remarkable text, nevertheless, which Lukàcs was to repudiate only reluctantly; it may have influenced Max Scheler as well as Mannheim.[22] Lukàcs observes that "... historical materialism cannot be applied in the same way to pre-capitalist structures and to capitalist development";[23] its pre-capitalist applications become blurred or specious when the past is delved into; when the power of the proletariat came on the scene, it ushered in the beginning of "a new form of validity" of this principle (a form remarkably similar to *a cessation of validity*). In fact, in the socialist context, with the appearance of social planning, the political sphere regains its former primacy and the economy, having lost "its immanence, autonomy, and everything that made it an economy"[24] comes to be eliminated as an economy.[25] With the well-known leap into the realm of freedom, Marxism causes itself to be eliminated as it comes into being; the transition period is the reign of "politics first," to use a very well-known expression that is not exactly Marxist in origin. (It comes from Charles Maurras, well known royalist theorist and leader in France.) It is thus true that beyond the differences between left- and right-wing politics, authoritarianism as such has permanent ideological structures.

According to Lukàcs and his followers, the validity of historical materialism should as a result be limited to a rather short period of history: that of capitalist reification. Reification "naturalizes" the laws of capitalist economy; such an elevation of social laws — albeit illusory — to the level of natural laws[26] is expressed precisely by the postulate of the validity of economic determinism during a limited historical period. In precapitalist societies characterized by a feeble degree of reification, this determinism is of limited validity; the same holds true for postcapitlist ("socialist") societies where the victorious political action of the working class has broken the iron ring of capitalist reification. This is the famous "leap" from servitude to freedom.

Lukàcs, Mannheim, and Scheler, each from his own personal point of view, all adopted this hypothesis, which orthodox Marxism has always refused to express clearly. However, for Lukàcs this "leap" can only be created historically by the proletariat; for Mannheim, it could come about within the framework of democratic planning. Lukàcs adds that it is only in the light of an awareness of the historical (and as such transitory and relative) nature of capitalist reification that we are in position to understand the essence of societies and cultures anteriors to the emergence of capitalism. The simultaneous rise of Marxism and of the sociology of the so-called primitive societies is not an accident.[27] An uncritical application of the notion of the primacy of economic factors to precapitalist eras is born of vulgar Marxism; "the use of historical materialism has fallen into the error for which Marx criticized vulgar economics; it has mistaken historical categories, those of capitalist society, for eternal categories."[28]

This point of view was taken up by Mannheim — and to be frank, with no great originality. His formulations are sometimes more propitious than those of Lukàcs. In his polemic against Scheler, Mannheim developed the idea that there is advantage to reconstruct historical wholes ("historical totalities" according to the terminology of Lukàcs) from their infrastructures and in particular from their "production relations" (*Produktionsverhältnisse*) as a basis, since at the contemporary stage of historical evolution there is effectively a shift in the "accent of reality" toward these relations. However the further one goes back in time, from capitalism towards precapitalist systems, the more the applications of traditional historical materialism become hazy.

It is undeniable that these developments carry the clear influence of a reading of *History and Class Consciousness*, but the importance of Mannheim's borrowings from Lukàcs should not be overemphasized either, considering the differing overall orientations of their works. In 1923, Lukàcs was before all a militant philosopher, writing from the point of view of class and the party. Mannheim, a sociologist and an academic, was only later to give his support to Anglo-Saxon democracy; during his German period, he enjoyed a virtually independent situation in relation to the class struggle. He not only advocated "freischwebende Intelligenz," he was, at that time, a typical representative of it. His "Standort" in 1929 allowed a broader view of the problem of ideology than that afforded to a minister actively taking part in a revolutionary government. In the chapter in question, Lukàcs demonstrated that historical materialism is the superstructure of a certain form of society — capitalist society — which is at one and the same time its source and field of validity par excellence. Mannheim carried matters somewhat further. In his analysis of the total and general conception of ideology and in certain aspects of his description of Utopian consciousness, he perceived the guidelines of the mechanism that was used much later to set in motion the process of an ideologization of proletarian consciousness that was to culminate in Stalinism. Lukàcs shows that historical materialism is a *superstructure;* Mannheim perceives its possible transformation into an *ideology* symptomatic of false consciousness. That is not exactly the same thing.[29]

In fact, this attempt at precapitalist validation of the principle of historical determinism foreshadows another phenomenon which was one of the most curious manifestations of ideologization of historical sensitivity in Stalinism. We have in mind this phenomenon — or perhaps this technique — of sociocentric reevaluation of past events according to present needs and criteria, immortalized in George Orwell's *1984*. In collective egocentrism — as in all individual egocentrism — historical time is structured according to pragmatic, totally nonobjective criteria.[30] Both phenomena (retroactive application of historical materialism to pre-capitalist history and reevaluation ex post facto of historical facts) are two forms (or levels) of ideological anti-historicism. The following text by Lukàcs leaves little room for doubt: "All historical knowledge is knowledge of self. The past becomes clear only when auto-criticism of the present is set into motion. Until such time, the past must necessarily either *be naively identified with structural forms of the present* (!) or be completely beyond understanding and as such completely foreign, absurd, and barbarous."[31]

The meaning of this passage could not be any clearer. Only an auto-criticism of the present (*eine Selbstkritik der Gegenwart*), i.e. a critical transcedence of any idealization of the present state of events, allows for an understanding of the specificity of historical antecedents, or in other words, their *historicity*. When understood from an egocentric ("presentocentric") point of view and thereby imbued with an illusory primacy the present tends to assimilate the past, leading to a homogenization of historical time and even reducing it to a continuum of spatial structure. By asking and giving a negative answer to the question of the respective validity of economic determinism, Lukàcs and Mannheim gave an answer in anticipation to a different question that was to be raised only much later by the ideologization of historical sensitivity in Marxism under the hammer of Stalin and Jdanov.

In principle, Marxism has never been very much concerned by the problems of the psychology of the *individual*. "Marx," wrote Sydney Hook, "is not at all interested in the motives of individuals as such, except insofar as they symbolize a class attitude."[32] Considering the state of the science of psychology at that time, such a lack of interest is quite understandable.

Physiologism, which was so characteristic of Russian psychiatry at that time, resulted from two ultimately converging chains of causes. First, Marxism offers no psychology of the individual; Marxists such as psychiatrists among others, who are compelled to study individuals are, as a result, forced to turn back to pre-Marxist materialism. Second, by eliminating the social factor, organicism in psychiatry can be used to clear the supposedly perfect socialist reality of any suspicions of pathogenic action.

In principle, for Marxism, it is social being that determines consciousness. It is here that Marxism finds itself at a dead end. Either it has to support simultaneously an epiphenomenalist theory of morbid consciousness and a dialectical theory of normal consciousness, or to limit the valid scope of the determination of social consciousness to the collective contents of consciousness (class consciousness), which in the end would be an avowal of Marxism's total failure in the psychology of the individual. The problem of pathological consciousness becomes therefore the litmus test of dialectical materialism's viability as a synthesis of two doctrines of different origins. Philosophers may play with verbal syntheses; a Marxist psychiatrist confronted with the concrete problems of pathological consciousness is compelled to make some choice: either materialistic physiologism with no relation to dialectics, or dialectical sociologism far removed from materialism. Now unlike traditional Marxism, the conceptions of Lukàcs and Mannheim involve a genuine individual dimension which is potentially a psychiatric one. I tried to demonstrate that point with respect to Lukàcs when stressing the clinincal value of the notion of reified consciousness.[33] Mannheim's notion of "socially determined thought" is in practical terms the same as that which dominates the studies of the existential school of analysis (Binswanger), an authentic sociology of knowledge of delirious thought[34] and undoubtedly the psychopathological school, closest to historical materialism. Pathological consciousness is the stumbling block for scholastic Marxism.

It is noteworthy that the Marxism of Mannheim, in the same way as that of Lukàcs, is capable of surmounting that problem.

"Of all Marxist theories," writes Hook, "the materialist conception of History is the most often misunderstood. It is to be ascribed not only to the ambiguity of some of the most important expressions, but also to the fact that Marx considered it to be a method of analyzing and making history, whereas his disciples wanted to change it into a system of sociology. That is why its flexibility in the writings of Marx and Engels ends up being sacrificed to an unverifiable dogma in the works of their followers."[35] I should add to this apparently accurate diagnosis that Marx and Engels are in part responsible for such misunderstandings by applying the term "materialist" to a doctrine that has little to do with ontological materialism as well as by failing to give a global and coherent account of their theory involving unambiguous definitions. In this philosophical question, the attitude of Marx and Engels was dictated as much by their preoccupations as militants as by those as theorists. The clarity of their overall system could not help but suffer.

"It is Marx and I in part," writes Engels, "who must bear the blame for the fact that the young sometimes overestimate the importance of economic factors. When confronted with our adversaries, we had to stress the essential principle denied by them, and we not always found the time or place or the opportunity to give space to the other factors involved in reciprocal action."[36] This explains the flourishing of many pseudo-Marxist theories such as the technological interpretation of history by Bogdanov (which influenced Bukharin), historical monism and, above all, a pseudo-materialism in the style of Helvetius, which considers *economic interest* to be both the prime moving force of history and the main factor in the process of ideologization. The history of ideas has seldom known a doctrine subject to so many contradictory interpretations.

In the present study, I have posited a working hypothesis that all Marxist theory has dualist structure: *dialectical sociologism* and *economic determinism*. These are two *ideal types* that, as such, have not been the object of precise formulation. The conceptions of Lukàcs and Mannheim are fairly close to the first type and those of Bukharin to the second. As for the definitions made by Marx and Engels, they are polyvalent, and it is possible to draw whatever one will from them. The belief in the illusory homogeneity of Marx's doctrine has always been a factor of ideologization.

Calvez was not wrong in considering the famous preface to Marx's *Zur Kritik der politischen Okonomie* to be tainted with "unilateral and equivocal determinism."[37] The letters of Marx and Engels, in which the economic factor comes into play only in the final analysis,[38] seem on the contrary to be in line with dialectical sociologism. Moreover, the expression "final analysis" is full of ambiguity. In the debate on whether mental illnesses are due to psychic or organic causes, the question is not to know whether an "organic sub-stratum" does exist or not in the final analysis, which nobody would think of calling into question (insanity cannot exist without a brain), but whether the autonomous dynamics of the psychic sphere may become pathogenic. The problem of economic infrastructure is posed — in the same terms. There is no need to be a Marxist to admit that laws completely incompatible with the economic system will not survive for long; the economic factor is therefore what decides "the final analysis." If historical materialism were nothing more than that, non-Marxist historians could be counted on the fingers of one hand. The notion of "final analysis" echoes the dismissive nod that well-bred theorists seldom refuse when bidding farewell to some doctrinal conception. It is sufficient to disregard it, and the letters of Marx and Engels throw us back into the climate of dialectical sociologism. It is no coincidence therefore, that those letters contain one of the rare passages in which Marx uses the *total concept of ideology* in Mannheim's meaning of the term.[39] Nor is it a coincidence if the few attempts to draw Marx and Durkheim together were predominated by the issue of alienation and ended up pointing out a critical theory of ideology implicit in Durkheimism.[40]

With regard to historical materialism, Mannheim was not in the end highly innovative. The importance of his attempt is situated on another level. His procedure calls to mind that of a chemist succeeding in isolating two isomers from an apparently homogeneous chemical substance. He is one of those who perceived — albeit his theory was not clearly formulated — the fundamental dualist structure of Marxism, and drew the conclusions of that insight by opting unambiguously on all levels for *dialectical sociologism of de-alienation*. The potential opening of his thought to the problems of individual alienation is the fruit of that choice, devoid of all compromise. Among all the varying forms of present-day Marxism, Mannheim's conception is the one that presents the most coherent doctrinal whole against authoritarian Marxism.

But was he really Marxist? There is disagreement on the matter, although there are weighty arguments on all sides. This is a characteristic of the intellectual fate of a thinker who often "thought against." It is the defenders of orthodox Marxism, such as Fogarasi and Lukàcs in his latter period, who refused to call him a Marxist, though others, reserved in their acceptance of Marxism, tended to call him one. Both Marxists and anti-Marxists have tended to shunt Mannheim from one side to the other; for those who appreciate heretical thought, this could well be a recommendation. Like R. Aron, I prefer to consider Mannheim as the representative of a "peculiar Marxism both spiritualist and relativist"[41] which could also be a Marxism of demystification.[42]

This "peculiar Marxism" had a number of adepts in Weimar Germany; using the name of "Western Marxism," it knew its hour of glory in France. After the deaths of Merleau-Ponty, Goldmann, and Sartre, it lost importance in the face of the great competition of the Althusser school. As for Mannheim, he was a latecomer; in 1956, the issue of the end of the ideological era was on the agenda.

This is no longer the case. The works on the problem of ideology are burgeoning and the concept of false consciousness is emerging from a no-man's-land (or, if it is preferred, a refugee camp) between scholastic Marxism, which rejected it as a possible instrument of a rather undesirable de-mystification, and "bourgeois" intellectual life, which is suspicious because of its "suspect" origins. I have even found the term in the columns of Le Figaro![43] Whether ideologized or not, false consciousness is far from being absent in the contemporary political scene. Mannheim's work, Diagnosis of Our Time, was published in 1943, yet the above-quoted passages might have been written yesterday.[44] Our epoch is marked with the stamp of "social amnesia." Now such amnesia naturally promotes an a-historical perception of political events and, in consequence, the rise of false consciousness. At a time when a considerable fraction of the world's black peoples paradoxically pledge allegiance to Hitler, who refused to shake hands with a black Olympic champion in 1936, Mannheim's de-mystifying and historicist Marxism — de-mystifying because historicist — still has something relevant to say.

## Notes

1. "....eine radikale Entökonomisierung," Lukàcs, *Die Zerstörung der Vernunft* (Berlin: 1955), 522. This is one of the many hasty judgements made about Mannheim in orthodox Marxist circles.
2. Cf. the formula by Lukàcs: It is not the predominance of economic issues in the explanation of history that makes the distinctive difference between Marxism and "bourgeois" science, it is rather the point of view of totality. G. Lukàcs, *History and Class Consciousness* (Paris: Ed. de Minuit, 1961), 39.

   These two texts are similar, but it seems that this break with the principle of unilateral economic determinism is only sketched by G. Lukàcs.
3. G. Gurvitch, "Le problème de la sociologie de la connaissance," *Revue Philosophique 1958-1959*.
4. R. Meigniez, "L'Univers de la culpabilité. Réflexions sur les bases du stalinisme intellectuel en Europe," *Psyché* (Paris) (April 1952). Karl Korsch, *Marxismus und Philosophie* (Berlin: Malik Verlag, 1923); and Francfort & Vienna: Europaische Verlaganstalt, 1972; French edition: *Marxisme et Philosophie*, Paris, Editions de Minuit, 1964, with a preface of Kostas Axelos (Collection "Arguments"). See: Gabel, *Ideologies*, Paris, Editions Anthropos 1974, 149–64 (Korsch, Lukàcs et le problème de la conscience de classe) and 79–106 (Psychologie du stalinisme) published as an article in 1949.
5. In this way, racism is not an ideology because it points out the existence of ethnic inequalities but only as far as it considers such inequalities as definitive (an-historism) and solely dependent on biology (a-sociologism).
6. B. Fogarasi, *Marxizmus ès Logika* (Budapest: Szikra, 1946), 164 ff.
7. S. Hook, *Pour comprendre Marx* (Paris: Gallimard, 1936), 197.
8. J.Y. Calvez, *La Pensée de Karl Marx* (Paris: Gallimard, 1936).
9. Lukàcs, *History,* 198.
10. J. Lacroix, *Le personnalisme comme anti-idéologie* (Paris: P.U.F., 1972).
11. R.K. Merton, *Karl Mannheim and the Sociology of Knowledge,* and J. Maquet, Chap. 9 note 8.
12. The references are made to the fourth German edition of *Ideology and Utopia* (1965) and the 1936 English edition.
13. English edition (E), p. 144; original (O), p. 141.
14. "E" p. 54; "O" p. 58.
15. "E" p. 72; "O" p. 73.
16. "E" p. 76; "O" p. 77.
17. "E" p. 148; "O" p. 146.

18. "E" p. l99; "O" p. 192.
19. "E" p. 223; "O" p. 214.
20. Lukàcs, *History*, (translated by Axelos-J.Bois) 257 ff.
21. Contrary to widespread opinion in the West, the head of the Hungarian Communist government in 1919 was not Béla Kun but A. Garbai.
22. Max Scheler made out three orders of "real factors" (Realfaktoren): each alternately exerted a determining historical action "in the final analysis": the factors of blood, power, and politics (Scheler, *Die Wissensformen und die Gesellschaft* [Leipzig, 1926], 370.) Such a curious widening of the field of historical materialism would call for a gnoseo-sociological analysis which would be at the same time psychoanalytical.
23. Lukàcs, *History*, 274.
24. Ibid., 275.
25. Note this curious idea: Lukàcs believed that a reified economy ceases to be an economy.
26. Here is another example which, though overused, is indispensable for the understanding of the problem: the theory of the Victorian economist W. Jevons who explained the periodicity of economic crises by the periodicity of the appearance of sunspots.
27. Lukàcs, *History,* 274.
28. Ibid., 275.
29. Cf. this completely characteristic passage: "Whereas in class struggles of the past, the greatest variety of ideologies, religions, moral, and other forms of false consciousness were decisive, the proletarian class struggle, the emancipating war of the last oppressed class, found, in the revelation of truth discovered, both the call to combat and its most efficient weapon" (Lukàcs, *History,* 258–9).

    That is clear, as is the necessary conclusion: *Lukàcs was wrong.* Mannheim did not share that illusion. Despite the disturbingly similar terminology, Mannheim's philosophy of de-alienation, which resulted from the convergence of ideas of Lukàcs and Paul Szende (cf. Paul Szende, "Mystification and Demystification," in Gabel, Rousset, Trinh Van Thao, *L'Aliénation d'aujourd'hui* [Paris: Anthropos, 1974], 319-48) is dialectically ahead of both of them.
30. See the quoted article by Honorio Delgado, chap. 7, note 20.
31. Lukàcs, *History*, translation (see note 20), 273.
32. S. Hook, *Pour comprendre Marx* (Paris: Gallimard, 1936).
33. See my article on reification in psychopathology, *Esprit,* 1951, reprinted in *Sociologie de l'Alienation* (Paris: P.U.F., 1970), 136–61.
34. Binswanger deduces the structure of a psychosis or neurosis from the structure of the individual's adaptation to the community (Dasein). Thus, in the case of a young girl who has failed to synthesize her dissipated

youth and well-ordered maturity, the dissociation in her past life takes on the form of a psychosis of dissociation (a case of L. Binswanger). Despite his somewhat "idealist" terms (such as Dasein), his theory remains a genuine sociology of knowledge of pathological thought; the term of "socially determined delirious thought" *(Seinsverbundenes Wahndenken)* is unavoidable. The advantage of Mannheim's interpretation of historical materialism is that it allows for such openness to individuals, whereas orthodox Marxism's blindness to psychology obliged Marxist psychiatrists either to turn to mechanistic materialism (organogenesis) or to Pavlovian psychology, a valuable theory which, however, has nothing to do with dialectics.

35. S. Hook, *Pour comprendre,* 99.
36. "Engels à Bloch," in *Etudes philosophiques* (Paris: Editions sociales, 1951), 130.
37. Calvez, *La pensée de Karl Marx* (Paris: Seuil, 1956), 424.
38. Marx and Engels, *Etudes philosophiques,* 128, 137.
39. Letter from Marx to Annenkov, Ibid., 123: "Even less did Mr. Proudhon understand that the men who fashion social relations in conformity with their mode of material production, also fashion ideas, categories, that is to say abstract, ideal expressions of those very social relations."
40. Cf. Gabel, "Durkheimianism and political alienation. Durkheim and Marx," *The Canadian Journal of Sociology,* vol. 9, no. 2, 1984.
41. R. Aron, *Sociologie allemande,* 83.
42. I have already mentioned Mannheim's misunderstood indebtedness to P. Szende, the author of *Verhüllung und Enthüllung.*
43. In issue no. 28 (October 1982), Pascal Salin warned against the danger of false consciousness. On October twentieth of that year B. Bonilauri spoke of the false consciousness distorting the perception of Soviet life in western countries. It is highly meaningful that a Marxist concept appeared in a resolutely anti-Marxist newspaper: *false consciousness has changed sides.* The "Western" world is now more open to a form of demystifying thought than is the socialist world.
44. Cf. chap. 7, note 20.

# Bibliography

Aron, R. *Contemporary German Sociology.* Paris, P.U.F., 1950.
_____ . Ideology, *Recherches Philosophiques,* 1936/37.
Ascoli, M. "On Mannheim's Ideology and Utopia." *Social Research,* February, 1938.
Becker, H., & Dahlke, O. "Max Scheler's Sociology of Knowledge." *Philosophy and Phenomenological Research,* 1941/42.
Bloch, E. *Thomas Münzer, Theologian of the Revolution.* Paris, 1962.
Fogarasi, B. *Introduction to Marxist Philosophy.* Vienna, 1922.
_____ . *Conservative Idealism and Progressist Idealism.* In *Twentieth Century.* Budapest, 1917.
_____ . *Marxism and Logic,* Budapest, 1946, followed by "Karl Mannheim's Sociology and Dialectical Method."
Gabel, J. "The Mannheim Problem in France." *Newsletter of the International Society for the Sociology of Knowledge,* August, 1983.
_____ . "Lucien Goldmann, a Reader of Karl Mannheim." *Kölner Zeitschrift für Soziologie und Sozialpsychologie,* sp. issue, 1980/22.
Gabor, E., *Critique of Mannheim's Conception of Utopia,* (in Hungarian). Publications of the Institute for Research in Marxism-Leninism of the Budapest Polytechic School, 1977. "Mannheim and Dialectics," in Gabel et al., *Actualité de la Dialectique.* Paris: Anthropos, 1980. "Mannheim in Hungary & Weimar Germany," *Newsletter of the International Society for the Sociology of Knowledge,* 1983.
Goldmann, L. *The Human Sciences and Philosophy.* Paris: P.U.F., 1952.
Grünwald, E. *The Problem of the Sociology of Knowledge.* Leipzig, 1934.
Gurvitch, G. "The Problem of the Sociology of Knowledge." *Revue Philosophique,* 1958/59.
Guttmann, F. "Paul Szende's Scientific Activity between 1919 and 1934" (in Hungarian) *Our Century* (Budapest), November 1934.
Horowitz, I.L. Mannheims Wissenssoziologie und C.W. Mill's soziologisches Wissen *Kölner Zeitschrift für Soziologie und Sozialpsy-*

*chologie* 1980, Special issue no. 22. (The Sociologie of Knowledge and Mannheim and the sociological culture according to C.W. Mills.)

Jaszi, O. "Inductive Verification of Historical Materialism." In Gabel et al., *Alienation Today*. Paris: Anthropos, 1974. pp. 349-63.

Kettler et al. *Karl Mannheim*. London & New York: Tavistock, 1984.

Kolnai, A. "Erroneous Conscience." *Proceedings of the Aristotelician Society*, February 1958.

_____. "Notes on Reactionary Utopia." *Cité Libre* (Montreal), November 1955.

Lenk, K. "Karl Mannheim." *Handwörterbuch der Sozialwissenschaften.*

Lewalter, E. "Sociology of Knowledge and Marxism." *Archiv für Sozialwissenschaft und Sozialpolitik* (1930) 64.

Mannheim, E. "Karl Mannheim." *The American Journal of Sociology*, May 1947.

Mannheim, K. "Beiträge zur Theorie des Weltanschauung-Interpretation." *Jahrbuch für Kunstgeschichte*, T. 57, 1927.

_____. "Conservative Thinking. Sociological Contributions to the Growth of Politico-historical Thinking in Germany." *Archiv für Sozialwissenschaft und Sozialpolitik*, T. 57, 1927.

_____. "The Generation Gap." *Kölner Vierteljahrshefte für Soziologie*, 1928.

_____. "The Problem of a Sociology of Knowledge." *Archiv für Sozialwissenschaft und Sozialpolitik*, 1925.

_____. *Diagnosis of our Time*. New York: Oxford University Press, 1944.

_____. The Meaning of Competition in the Realm of the Mind." Paper for the 6th Congress of German-speaking Sociologists, Zürich, 1928.

_____. *Presentday Tasks of Sociology*. Tübingen, 1932. "Reason and Passion in Contemporary Society" (in Hungarian). Századunk, Budapest, April 1934.

_____. *Essays on Sociology & Social Psychology*. New York: Oxford University Press, 1953.

_____. *Essays on the Sociology of Knowledge* (with introduction by P. Kecskeméti). London: Routledge & Kegan Paul, 1952.

_____. *Freedom Power & Democratic Planning*. New York: Oxford University Press, 1950.

_____. "Historismus." *Archiv für Sozialwissenschaft und Sozialpolitik*, T. 52, 1924.

_____. *Ideology and Utopia*. Frankfurt: Schulte-Bulmke Verlag, 1965; English translation by E. Wirth and e. Shils. London: Routledge &

Kegan Paul, 1936.

_____ . "Ideological and Sociological Interpretation of Mental Structures." *Jahrbuch für Soziologie,* Karlsruhe, 1926.

_____ . *Soul and Culture*    (in Hungarian). Budapest, 1918.

_____ . *Man and Society in an Age of Reconstruction.* Leiden, 1935. The English translation (London and New York, 1940 and 1954) contains hitherto unpublished chapters.

_____ . *Preliminary Approach to the Problem.* Preface to the English edition of *Ideology and Utopia).*

_____ . "Reason and Passion in Contemporary Society" (in Hungarian). Budapest: Szazdunk, April 1934.

_____ . "Structural Analysis of Epistemology" (Kant-Studien) No 57, 1922.

_____ . "Utopia." *Encyclopaedia of the Social Sciences.* New York, 1935.

_____ . "Sociology of Knowledge." *Handwörterbuch für Soziologie* (A. Vierkandt). Stuttgart, 1931.

_____ . *Sociology of Knowledge.* Berlin-Neuwied, 1964. (Re-edition of Mannheim's main essays with an introduction by Kurt Wolff).

Maquet, J. *Sociology of Knowledge.* Louvain: E. Neuwelaerts, 1949.

Ruyer, R. *Utopia and Utopias.* Paris, P.U.F., 1950.

Scheler, M. *Die Wissensformen und die Gesellschaft.* Leipzig: Neuer Geist Verlag, 1926.

_____ . *Versuche zu einer Soziologie des Wissens.* Munich/Leipzig: Duncker & Humbot Verlag, 1924.

Simonds, A.P. *Karl Mannheim's Sociology of Knowledge.* Oxford: Clarendon Press, 1978.

Speier, H. "Review of Ideology & Utopia by Karl Mannheim." *American Journal of Sociology,* July 1957.

_____ . "The Social Determination of Ideas." *Social Research,* May 1958.

Stark, W. *The Sociology of Knowledge. An Essay in Aid of a Deeper Understanding of the History of Ideas.* Glencoe, Ill.: The Free Press, 1958.

Szabo. E. *Free Trade and Imperialism.* Graz, 1918.

_____ . *Social and Party Struggles during the Hungarian Revolution of 1948/49* (in Hungarian). Vienna, 1921, and Budapest, 1945 (with an extremely critical preface by Joseph Révai).

_____ . *Imperialism and Durable Peace* (in Hungarian). Budapest, 1917.

_____ . *Selected Works by Marx and Engels,* (edition with commentary by E. Szabo). Budapest, 1905-1909.

_____ . "On the Possibility of a Scientific Policy." *Huszadik Szàzad*, January-June 1910.

_____ . "On the Jewish Question." *Huszadik Szàzad*, July-August 1917.

Szende, P. "Sociological Theory of Abstraction." *Archiv für Sozialwissenschaft und Sozialpolitik*, April 1923.

_____ . *Mystification and Demystification. The Struggle of Ideologies in History.* Leipzig: Hirschfeld Verlag, 1922. French translation in part in Gabel et al., *Alienation Today.* Paris: Anthropos, 1974. Pp. 319-48 (translation by R. Eucher and G. Villa).

Wittfogel, K.A. "Knowledge and Society. Recent German Literature on the Sociology of Knowledge." *Unter dem Banner des Marxismus*, An. V. fasc. I.

Woldring H. *Karl Mannheim. The Developoment of His Thought.* 1986 ed. Van Gorcum, Maastricht (Holland).

Wolff, Kurt. *From Karl Mannheim.* New York: Oxford University Press, 1971.

Wright-Mills, C. "Death of Ideologies." *Les Lettres Nouvelles*, February 1971.